The Cricket Conspiracy

by Derek Humphry

*With an introduction by Hugo Young
and an appendix by Geoff Robertson*

National Council for Civil Liberties

The National Council for Civil Liberties is an independent, voluntary organisation, protecting individual civil liberties and the rights of political, racial and other minorities in Britain. Founded in 1934, the NCCL is financed solely by membership fees and donations. Its membership is drawn from those who are increasingly anxious about encroachments on civil liberties.

Part of the NCCL's work is to campaign for legal reforms and recent campaigns conducted nationally and by local groups have concerned the administration of justice in Northern Ireland, the need for an independent police complaints machinery, the reform of the law on picketing and demonstrations, and the individual's right to privacy.

Where possible, the NCCL investigates grievances and allegations of injustice. It submits evidence to government enquiries, briefs MP's and peers for Parliamentary debates and questions, publishes pamphlets on major civil liberty issues, and mobilizes public opinion, through press, radio and television.

The NCCL depends on the support and help of its member and affiliates to accomplish a growing amount of work. A membership form is included on the last page of this book. If you aren't already a member of NCCL, we encourage you to join us now.

ISBN 0 901108 40 5

Copyright © May 1975 National Council for Civil Liberties
NCCL, 186 Kings Cross Road, London WC1X 9DE. Telephone - 01-278 4575
Printed by The Russell Press Ltd., 45 Gamble Street, Nottingham. Telephone: 0602-74505

Hugo Young   is Political Editor of the
Sunday Times, London

Derek Humphry   is a staff reporter on the *Sunday
Times* specialising in civil
liberties and race relations.

Geoff Robertson   is a barrister practising
chiefly in cases involving
civil liberties.

In memory of Jean Humphry
Always a campaigner

Contents

Foreword

Three years have passed since the trial of Peter Hain for conspiracy to stop the white South African rugby and cricket tours of Britain, yet the case remains a landmark in the history of protest and the law of conspiracy.

Publication of this boook was delayed by time taken to reach the appeal in the case of R.V. Kamara (the Sierra Leone Embassy take-over) which was crucial to the law of conspiracy to trespass. Thus the final adjudication of the Hain case awaited the Kamara judgement . . . and the wheels of justice turn slowly.

By the time we were ready to publish an economic blizzard had hit the printing world, adding greatly to our problems, but it has been worth the wait to get on record one of the most curious trials in modern times which was the aftermath of the mass Stop-The-Seventy-Cricket-Tour campaign.

The evidence of the trial has many interesting aspects. Amongst them are the first full accounts of how it feels to be demonstrated against (in the words of the Springbok rugby players) and the declarations of the moral philosophy of the people who took quite uncharacteristic actions to show their abhorrence of racialism.

London, March, 1975.   *Derek Humphry*

Introduction

by Hugo Young

The campaign organised in 1969 and 1970 against sporting relations between Britain and South Africa was the most successful pressure-group action in recent British political history. It had two objectives. It achieved, or began to achieve, both of them, and did so almost instantaneously. First it sought the isolation of South Africa in world sport, and in particular the severing of all relations between Britain and South African sporting bodies. Secondly, it sought, as a result of the inconvenience and displeasure such isolation caused in South Africa, to bring about a fundamental change in sporting, and ultimately political practices there. Although this second objective remains a long way from being attained, important changes have occurred which indicate the beginning of a process which the South African government cannot now interrupt with impunity.

It is hard to think of a single large political campaign which has had anything like so immediate an impact. Other pressure groups which have toiled for years against such bottomless social evils as bad housing (Shelter) and poverty (Child Poverty Action Group) must look with envy on this extraordinarily swift international triumph.

Success was bought, however, only at a price. The campaign was pursued by unorthodox methods. It aroused intense political opposition, culminating in an accidental coincidence with the 1970 General Election. It provoked a lot of prosecutions and the beginnings of an important debate about the legitimacy of illegal activities in the pursuit of political objectives. Finally this debate was crystallised in the course of a major trial prosecuted by a private citizen, Francis Bennion, against the main organiser of the campaign, a South African exile named Peter Hain.

This is a book not so much about the campaign itself — although some details of it inevitably feature largely in what follows — as about the aftermath. Centrally there is the trial of Hain, which provides a record of that relatively rare spectacle in British courts, a dispute about political methods and objectives. That was not all the trial was about, and not the ground on which the jury had to decide whether Hain was guilty of conspiracy. But the legal argument was conducted against the constant background of an argument about political and moral principle.

Secondly, the trial raised once again in modern English law the validity of using the conspiracy laws where statute fails to supply a ground for prosecution. In several sensitive areas of human activity, of which obscene publication is the most prominent, the police have resorted to conspiracy charges to bring to court people who might otherwise remain untouched by the law. In the Hain case, the police explicitly refused to bring such a prosecution. It was left to a private citizen to do so but he was doubtless encouraged in this by the knowledge that policemen and jurists, from the House of Lords down, have been willing to give to conspiracy a very modern incarnation.

7

Bennion's action was finally concluded only in 1973. Until that moment it was not possible to examine the trial with detachment. Although there have been more recent developments in the sporting boycott of South Africa, the events which caused the trial happened more than five years ago. They need to be briefly recalled before a discussion of the fundamental argument which gave rise to the trial, and which remains a pressing one for the democratic system.

Hain's campaign was called Stop the Seventy Tour (STST), and its purpose was to persuade the cricket authorities in Britain to call off a tour by the South African cricket team organised for the summer of 1970. Beginning in 1969, Hain and his friends dedicated themselves to mobilising public opinion against the cricket tour, and to showing what might happen if it did take place. To this end they used not only conventional arguments, reasoned statements and traditional demonstrations of strength but also more perilous methods. In particular two tours in 1969 became a focus for the campaign. An unofficial cricket tour, by the Wilf Isaacs team, and the official tour by the national rugby team, the Springboks, were the object of direct physical intervention, to stop games taking place or to challenge spectators watching them. The weapons of protest varied. They included establishing a mass presence at the grounds, running on to the field of play, sitting down there, distracting players on the field. Some protesters went further by carving up cricket pitches, but STST always made clear that this was not part of its own campaign. Throughout the rugger tour, the players suffered ceaseless harassment off the field, with various forms of social annoyance being perpetrated at their hotels. Throughout, there were many convictions for breaches of the peace and other minor offences.

But they were only preliminary to the real objective. Although valid enough in their own right, their most impressive impact was to show the conditions to which the cricket tour would be subject if it took place. Cricket is a gentle game, requiring time and tranquility. The fragile trance which it induces in spectators is utterly different from the raucous atmosphere of an international rugby match. Protests and incursions may infuriate rugger spectators and briefly interrupt the game but they cannot stop it unless deployed by vastly larger groups than STST ever tried to organise. Far from destroying the texture of an infinitely delicate spectacle, they almost amplify a rowdy one like rugger. Cricket, by contrast, can be rendered unpleasant and, quite quickly, impossible by any determined intervention. The STST campaign clearly hoped to demonstrate a strength of feeling against the 1970 cricket tour — with all its implications, as they saw it, for British complicity in the perpetuation of apartheid — as to make it not worth undertaking. They proposed to act within the law but they were willing, if necessary, to infringe it, while absolutely rejecting primary violence.

The cricket authorities, aware of their vulnerability, moved from early intransigence to a more defensive, though far from concessive, position. They planned to confine the tour to a few well-guarded grounds, instead of the customary progress round exposed and indefensible county fields. Barbed wire and other protections were placed around the chosen venues. For a time, the MCC was prepared to fight for cricket even if this meant turning Lords, Headingley and The Oval into inpenetrable bunkers.

In this the MCC was acting not merely as the custodian of a sport. MCC spokesmen cast themselves as the true defenders of liberal values. They felt it would be morally wrong to concede to pressure and stood squarely on the old adage that politics and sport do not mix. This became the keynote of their campaign, as it has remained the main plank of the rugger players' platform when they are asked to defend their continued games with the Springboks.

The argument involves a lot of logic-chopping, as the MCC soon discovered. In fact it sounded very like a desperate piece of special pleading to clothe with principle actions which really spring from sectional desire and self-interest. The MCC itself actually acknowledged a quasi-political role, in defending its decision, by claiming that "bridge-building", not isolation, was the way to end apartheid. Cricket had the honesty to do what rugby has for a long time refused to do: admit the necessary intertwining between sport and politics. Once it had admitted that the only real argument could be between those who thought the political purpose better served by one method than another, MCC's position became as political as STST's. And, very broadly, this was reflected in the support which each side got at the political level. Just as STST mobilised most "progressive" opinion behind it, the MCC was backed by most "conservative" opinion, in a grand dispute which raised issues not just about sport, but about law and freedom, morality and politics.

Cricket remained adamantly determined to put the tour on, and it was left to the Government as the guardian of the peace, to intervene and change the MCC's mind. Before the tourists had arrived and just before the General Election, Mr. Callaghan, then Home Secretary, asked Lord's to call it off, and Lord's obeyed. The reason why this decision was made was, it should be frankly admitted, not that Hain's arguments were so overwhelmingly persuasive, nor that great masses of the public agreed with them, but the threat of social disorder, lasting for several months, if the tour did go ahead. Some people, not surprisingly, saw this as a fateful moment in recent politics: the success of forceful methods in determining a Government decision.

Before considering the legal and moral implications of this, the substantial consequences of the campaign should be recorded. These were very considerable. First, the most specific domestic outcome was a statement from the cricket authorities announcing a permanent change of attitude towards South Africa. Having admitted a socio-political role, as sponsor of major national sporting engagements, MCC now decided that isolation was the only honourable and effective way of fulfilling it. English cricket bound itself not to resume relations with South African cricket until substantial changes in the direction of non-racialism in team selection were visible: a painful and highly significant shift for cricket to make.

Secondly, the cancellation of the tour and the MCC statement influenced other sporting bodies. For many people, it crystallised attitudes which until then had remained a matter of anxious uncertainty. When one of the world's most conservative sporting bodies demands such radical terms for any resumption of sporting ties, the ground really has moved. Pressure from black countries had already excluded South Africa from the Tokyo and Mexico Olympics, in 1964 and 1968. The year 1970 saw many sporting bodies shut her out: the Olympic Movement itself, world gymnastics, world netball, world cycling, world tennis, world athletics among others. Several other sports have intensified the pressure since 1970, so that it is now quite exceptional for any publicised sport to be played internationally in or with South Africa.

Thirdly, however, the trend towards isolation began to effect changes in South African life at a speed which even militant campaigners did not anticipate. Political leaders there have begun to bend the rules of the apartheid society to appease the sport-starved white population. This is done only cautiously, and without knocking aside any of the fundamental pillars of the segregated State. But events have occurred which, five years ago, would have been unthinkable. In 1973, Games were held in Pretoria, covering a variety of sports, at which international performers were watched by an unsegregated crowd. A white boxer has fought a black in the professional ring. Those touring teams which have come have had games against coloured and black teams: a token and in many ways offensive gesture but again, in South African terms, offering the extraordinary spectacle of whites and non-whites in physical contest. All this, moreover, has come about against a background of major reform in South African sporting bodies. Although anti-apartheid campaigners have reason to view sports administrators with scepticism, the fact is that, for whatever reason, several major sporting leaders in South Africa are now among the most effective agitators for change there. A debate has been opened up which involves not merely fringe radicals and solitary Africans but people sometimes close to the white establishment.

This briefly indicates the history and effect of the boycott campaign, of which Peter Hain was the most prominent leader at the time it was having its most important effects. One result of it is that no political observer can now visit South Africa without an early reference being made — usually with a venomous curl of the lip — to Hain and his activities. On the political level, he has already achieved more than many parliamentarians get done in a lifetime.

The bitterness, however, was not confined to South Africa. As well as being a milestone in British pressure-group politics, STST became the focus of a great mass of decent concern and indecent vituperation.

The main count against it was perhaps that it was successful; had the tour gone ahead, no one can imagine that the lofty principles cited against Hain would have been quite so prominently paraded. Also there was Hain himself, whose youth and South African origins seemed to produce in some people an appetite for low-level personalised attacks. These minor aspects of the case can be left aside, as can the crude defences of the apartheid system which were quite often advanced by Hain's critics: indeed, there is a strong suspicion that many of those who backed the prosecution — though not Francis Bennion himself — were driven on less by principle than by a warmly favourable attitude to South Africa.

The trial was not about apartheid. It was about the legal, political and moral conundrum posed by unlawful activities committed in a good cause.

*   *   *

Observing the events of Summer 1970, many people formed the strong opinion that society should not permit itself to be pushed around by lawbreakers. On this view, the illegal activities of STST were, if allowed to pass without legal censure, the beginning of a deeper and more worrying social collapse. The demonstrator and the trespasser foreshadowed the anarchist and the gunman. People could not be allowed to use their own freedom under the law to interfere with the freedom of others. Nor could they be permitted to employ a series of illegal acts as a means of bringing pressure on Parliament or local authorities to change the law. Still less, on this argument, could one sanction anyone's right to commit illegalities in Britain in order to change the law six thousand miles away.

In this way the Hain trial became the medium for a serious argument which arises, in the modern age, not simply over sport and South Africa. Several other significant public events have provoked it. Squatters who take over empty property; local councillors who refused to comply with the Tory Housing Finance Act; protesters who block the traffic on busy streets in order to press their case for new traffic lights; trade unionists who defied the Industrial Relations Act; and, going further back, the Committee of 100 against nuclear weapons, for whom direct action consisted of sitting down in Whitehall. All these groups have claimed the right to break the law either as a matter of principle or as a means of compelling society to change. Elsewhere, the civil rights movement in the United States provided perhaps the classic example of such a right being invoked on behalf of a whole people.

But does this right exist? If it does, what are the limits to which it may justly be pushed? Is there a valid distinction, in justice, between illegal action which is a matter of conscience and that which has an ulterior social purpose? Is there also a valid distinction between illegal acts which are violent and those which are non-violent? Are illegal methods justified in a dictatorship but not in a democracy, and if so, how do we define the difference? Is the very existence of Parliament enough to render any illegal action injustifiable? Again, assuming we grant some moral right to break the law and take the consequences, are those who urge on the lawbreakers in the same moral position as them?

These are questions which have occupied moral philosophers for centuries. A great variety of answers has been suggested to them. In this brief space I wish to discuss their relevance in the modern age and at the political level, in a society living under English Law.

In one sense, the Hain trial is a confusing point to begin. For in the trial, as in all courts of law, the object of the defence was to establish innocence, not to justify guilt. Hain's purpose was to resist the conspiracy charge, not to plead that his campaign was politically or ethically justifiable. Although a reading of the trial provides a fascinating concrete illustration of all these enduring moral questions, they are raised more by implication than in open debate between Hain and his prosecutor. They were not the question the jury had to decide. Thus, although STST campaigners claimed a high moral and social right — even duty — to commit breaches of the peace, that did not deter them from using every available tool of the law to establish that they had not committed an illegal conspiracy.

They did not invite any *court* to endorse their right to break the law. And since courts are the place where the existence of legal rights is formally determined, one limit of the argument is clearly set. That is: when we talk about illegal action and its justification we are plainly *not* discussing any claim that what is illegal should be rendered legal, or that the courts should overlook a manifestly illegal act, deeming it to have been justifiable by some higher social criterion. Hain's claim has never been that what is law should suddenly become non-law. Critics of the role of direct action have sometimes demolished this grand claim as if it was the kernel of the argument. It is not.

Secondly, the Hain campaign was not an attempt to change the law by extra-parliamentary and illicit pressure. Another major ground on which it was sincerely attacked was that it threatened the orderly processes of law-making; as if Parliament was so delicate a plant that it could be crushed by illegal demonstrations at cricket and rugby grounds. Leaving aside this improbable premise, the truth is that STST was aimed at public, and mainly cricketing, opinion. It tried to influence and perhaps define the social context in which the final decision about the 1970 tour was taken. It was not seeking to overturn the law — there hardly was a law, as such, to be overturned, as Bennion's resort to common-law conspiracy charges indicates — but to influence a policy. This does not alter the argument about the means it chose, but it distinctly reduces the damage STST can seriously be accused of attempting to do to the democratic system.

Thirdly, discussion of the case has been bedevilled by a confusion between illegal and merely unorthodox methods of protest. Sweeping aside legal niceties, defenders of the tour — like defenders of property taken over by squatters — often try to mobilise support, on the grounds of illegality, against action whose actual illegality is very doubtful. For example, in 1970 the illegality of individual action in going on to a cricket pitch and interfering with play was disputed, without any clear conclusion. Even the most rabid opponents of STST were unable, when pressed, to be sure of the application of the law of trespass. Similarly, such ungentlemanly ploys as sitting in the stand and using the reflection of sun on a mirror to dazzle a batsman fell in grey legal ground. Yet this did not deter the Tour's defenders from fulminating grandly against "law-breakers". Their readiness to stigmatise all inconvenient and bloody-minded activities as illegal reduced the impact of their claim to be preserving the very fabric of democratic society.

These three caveats are important. They show some of the many untidy edges of the argument. But the central case against Hain still stands and is not evaded by him or his supporters. It is, simply that illegality is never justified; must always be punished by society, preferably in a court; has no redeeming features, however laudable its objective may seem to many people. If attempts are made so to justify it, moreover, the very basis of public order and parliamentary democracy are in danger.

This is a clean and seemingly principled position. If it can be believed, it makes the judgement of particular cases very simple. But on inspection its clarity may be seen to conceal some troublesome difficulties.

For one thing, although an illegality cannot be made "legal" in a particular case — there is no legal *right* to break the law — that is not the same as saying that breaking the law is never justifiable. Plainly it *is* sometimes justifiable. A social decision is sometimes taken, which would attract common agreement, that someone who has broken the law — say, broken the speed limit to get a sick child to hospital — was justified in doing so. There are other occasions, often concerning matters of life and death, where the law is broken and neither policeman nor philosopher would deny that this was justified.

Furthermore, this erosion of the fundamental principle that lawbreaking is *never* justified is recognised and accelerated every day, by the custodians of the law itself. The "rule of law", to which the purist anti-Hain politicians often appealed in 1970, is corrupted by the manifest fact that the enforcement of law is highly selective. Law-breaking is not always investigated. When it is investigated it is not always brought to trial. When it is tried it is not always punished. Whenever a Chief Constable takes a discretionary decision not to prosecute an errant motorist, a chronic shoplifter or a pornographic bookseller he is taking a social decision that such conduct, which prima facie breaks the law, shall not in this case be formally designated and punished as "law-breaking".

Thus, pragmatism keeps polluting the pure concept of the rule of law. Society condones illegalities all the time. In doing so, it only reveals what is the fact — a hard fact for some people, and especially lawyers, to understand — that the law is not written in tablets resembling the Ten Commandments. The law is nothing more than a construct of rules which are convenient for society's better functioning, and which are never wholly static. Whatever statutes and textbooks may say, the law is in practice flexible. The social need for a law which is certain and fixed is counterbalanced by a social need that it should also sometimes be changed, ignored and even disobeyed.

Thus, if the enemies of the Hain campaign were right in their grand claim to be defending the integrity of society against an evil repudiation of the rule of law, then society should by now be under a great deal more peril than it really seems to be. For it turns out that many other people before Peter Hain have acted on the footing that to break the law was sometimes justifiable or would at least escape vengeance. Despite their efforts — judges, policemen, lawyers and moralists included — English society is intact. The *principle* of the divine and absolute rule is very frequently ignored. Yet society holds together; and does so, some would argue, rather more cohesively than it would if the principle became the one unalterable condition of political life.

But the principle was not consistently supported even by those who, in the Hain case, claimed to be defending it. They admitted that there were political circumstances in which law-breaking was permissible, namely in a dictatorship. But, they added, Britain, being the most perfect democracy in the world, with the freest rights of speech and assembly and the deepest respect for dissenters of every kind, is of all societies the one least likely to provide a justification for protest by unlawful means.

This is an important argument, but not surely, for the side most often making it. Quite rightly, those who offer it descend from the lofty plane of philosophy from which their argument starts. They say that there *are* circumstances in which the status quo — the law, the State — should not be able to claim an absolute defence against law-breakers. They argue that some systems are so utterly unjust that no moral duty of obedience exists. This is sensible enough. But it begs the very question the Hain trial posed: namely, the capacity of the British democratic system to respond to changing events and pressures, and to strong sectional feelings. Hain argued that there are situations in which orthodox democracy cannot meet the demands placed upon it, and that it may sometimes need to be supplemented by unorthodox methods, including if necessary unlawful ones.

Now, without urging everyone to go that far, it can surely be agreed that the democratic process in Britain is not the perfect instrument which Hain's antagonists find themselves having to claim. It has many shortcomings. MPs themselves, for example, worry constantly about the declining influence of Parliament and the growing power of the executive to achieve what it wants unchecked. The influence of the electorate on specific issues, via Parliament, is a matter of constant doubt. The whips, the disciplined two-party system, the sense of impotence between elections and even the sense of indifference at elections have all combined to maintain the moral authority of Parliament as the fount of action on every public question, and in particular its ability, in real life, to speak for the people as a whole. Far from being the work of an anarchistic minority, democratic reform and the modification of Parliamentary dominance is part of respectable public debate. It must qualify any assertion that British democracy is a system which it is totally unjustifiable to disturb as the single reliable arbiter of great disputes. Britain is obviously a long way from "dictatorship". But is the system so perfect that a rigid and static definition of the law is its best and only necessary defence?

It is the contention of those who passionately oppose Hain's activities that the system is of roughly that kind: and at the same time that it is fragile enough to be seriously threatened by illegal direct-action campaigns. Although their rhetoric is sometimes confused, they insist that there *is* a vital difference between the illegal and the merely unorthodox. There is, in their view, an essential distinction between something, however damaging, which is legal and something, however trivial, which is illegal. Society should fear and punish the second much more than the first. Bennion and others argue that the law sets the limit on human conduct, not necessarily because the law is good or modern or relevant or effective, but because it is the law. However imperfect the law is, to obey and uphold it is much less socially damaging than to break it and encourage others to break it.

As we have seen, this is not an argument which rests on high principle. It simply fails, at that level, to accord with the actual pattern of approved human conduct. So what about the practical level? Is the utilitarian and "political" argument against law-breaking as sound as its apologists seem to insist?

It rests on some sensible fears, which may be summarised as the "floodgates" argument. This fear is rooted very much in the particular nature of the lawbreaking, rather than the principle.

Although it is dressed up as a matter of the highest principle, the truth is that the hostility which the Hain campaign aroused against itself owed a lot to the particular nature of the law-breaking it involved and the particular issue, apartheid, to which it was directed. If STST had not involved *highly publicised* acts of law-breaking, had not had a *political* purpose and had not excited people's *strong hostility*, it would not have been very different from the many other acts of permitted law-breaking which go on every day in our society.

Both peculiarities of STST were equally significant. If its ultimate demand had not been for a clear political decision, to which end it was efficiently organised and sought a lot of publicity, its work would probably have been as little noticed as that of, say, the Festival of Light or the Anti-Apartheid Movement itself (which worked with the Hain campaign): continuing campaigns, engaged more in public education than in influencing any specific political decision. Similarly, if its purposes — to stop a cricket tour and to weaken apartheid — had not aroused a lot of people's rage, and had instead merely demanded their inert compliance (with, say, the proposition that world famine is bad), these great arguments of principle about law-breakers and what they could lead to might never have been pressed to a decision.

As it is, the success of the Hain campaign is said to have foreshadowed or intensified a long series of social evils: indiscipline on university campuses, blatant law-breaking by local councillors, five dockers defying the Industrial Relations Act, factory occupations by workers, even the Provisional IRA. It may not have been unique in undermining the rule of law, on this argument, but the particular form it took materially encouraged the declining respect for legality which many people perceive in British society.

This is a serious charge, but it is rather less serious than the claim that such actions as those taken by STST are never justified, or that freedom under the law is bound to be fatally damaged by them. The question is narrowed still further. It becomes, at bottom, a political question, about what kind of action is permissible in what kind of circumstances in response to what kind of grievance: rather than a question compelling those in Hain's position to justify — as prosecuting counsel regularly asked him to justify — other forms of illegal action in other circumstances. "Where would you draw the line?" he was insistently asked. The clear implication of this question is that once any unlawful action is sanctioned there is *nowhere* the line can be drawn. This means, in turn, that the unlawful action should never have begun and is absolutely unjustified. On this premise, merely asking the question is enough to establish the guilt of the man who has to answer it. But once the issue is seen as basically a political one, the question becomes less relevant; and the moral dilemma more resembles one which the individual and society must answer as each comes up.

This is surely the most realistic and helpful way to look at direct action and unlawful protest. It also takes account of history far more convincingly than the absolutist doctrine that illegal action is never justifiable. That doctrine offers no way of explaining historical developments of which those who preach it, anxious to show their liberal credentials, rarely claim to disapprove. Take the suffragettes in Britain and the civil rights campaign in the United States. Both were campaigns against long-standing imperfections in the democratic process which the democratic process, conventionally understood, failed to change. Both involved the commission of unlawful acts as a way of focussing public attention on these grievances and proving the determination of those who committed them to make personal sacrifices in return for political change. Both produced the desired effect, after the forces of the State had initially mobilised against them. Few of those who see the Hain campaign as a turning-point on the road to social chaos would now oppose the reforms those two campaigns directly brought about. How, then, can they continue to argue that unlawful actions must necessarily and in all circumstances be morally wrong as well as legally punishable?

What were the characteristics of the STST campaign, and what general rules of conduct did it observe? It was, first of all, non-violent. The primacy of non-violence has always been part of Hain's philosophy, as it was of Gandhi's and Martin Luther King's. Violence against either property or persons was rejected by the STST leaders, although that does not fortify their ethical position, in my view, so impregnably as Peter Hain sought to plead. The trouble with a populist and well-organised campaign, however non-violent, is that it produces secondary violence: either by hothead sympathisers, such as those who ripped up cricket pitches where South Africans were due to play, or by demonstrators and police in the clashes which became inevitable outside and inside rugby grounds in the winter of 1969-70. Campaign organisers cannot entirely exonerate themselves from the consequences of their acts.

Nonetheless it remains true that STST, unlike some other pressure-groups, sincerely wished to see no violence and worked to avoid it.

Secondly, STST readily accepted that participants would be punished. In that sense the demonstrations and other harassments were an act of individual conscience, bearing witness and making sacrifice against apartheid, as much as a lawless attempt to force the Government's hand. Although unwilling to lie down defenceless against the processes of law, the participants accepted without protest their legal penalties for breaches of the peace. (Complaints about police methods are a different matter.) They claimed no rights beyond those enjoyed by society at large. All they claimed was that they were entitled to break the law, and that it was ethically justifiable to do this and take the consequences.

Thirdly, STST was not a campaign using illegal methods against a decision arrived at by Parliament. It was not seeking to change the law or to repudiate, as a matter of conscience, some law passed with the full and mandated approval of Parliament (as many trade unionists repudiated the Industrial Relations Act). STST was directed against the decision of a tiny sectional oligarchy, the MCC, to sponsor a major, public, national event which had powerful political implications, since acknowledged and understood by the MCC itself. Although STST represented only a section of the public, it was not a section seeking to overturn the will of the majority. It was, rather, posing itself against the MCC, to make the country at large and the Government, see the cricket tour in a light in which it had not been widely seen before. As subsequent events have shown, this is a view of sport with South Africa which has come to command common support among most of Britain's, and the world's, sporting bodies.

These three qualities of Hain's campaign free it from the stigma which some would seal upon it. Together, in fact, they distinguish it from many other exercises in law-breaking for which justification has been prominently sought in recent years. The first — non-violence — totally differentiates it from the IRA and all other perpetuations of violence used to bring about political change. The second — a readiness to accept the penalties — distinguishes it from trade unionists who, in rejecting the Industrial Relations Act, also refused to pay them. The third — the object of the challenge — made STST very different from, for example, the Clay Cross councillors who refused to put the Housing Finance Act into practice. The councillors' conscience took them as far as defying, as a tiny minority, a clear and recent Act of Parliament, and demanding a Parliamentary amnesty from the consequences.

The justification or otherwise of each of those three exercises in law-breaking needs to be considered separately. Their very different features show only that, although illegal actions raise general philosophical questions, they must be considered, in practice, one by one in their special circumstances. There is no general and overwhelming duty to obey the law, rising above morality and personal conscience. And equally there is no general right to disobey the law as a personal gesture. The true liberation pretends neither that all law-breakers are wicked nor that all sincere law-breakers are good.

Less sweeping general rules are also hard to sustain. It has been argued that there is a difference between people who break laws out of conscience and those who do so an act of protest to change other laws or practices. Yet morally the former need be in no better position than the latter if his methods are violent; and the latter no worse than the former if he is willing to pay the penalty. Generalisations on this matter are, on the whole, made at peril and with alarming dialectical consequences.

It is safer to consider the particular case: its methods, its purposes and its results. People may differ in their view of the Hain campaign's purpose. But what his trial disclosed, I believe, was a protest movement whose methods and results were rooted in a highly respectable democratic tradition which, far from destroying British society, modernised and strengthened it. Also, by effecting a shift in British attitudes to a neglected issue it advanced the cause of non-racialism and improved Britain's standing in the world.

February, 1974.

CHAPTER 1

A Multi-Racial Jury

It took the clerk of the Court at the Old Bailey seven minutes to read the charges against Peter Hain on the afternoon of Thursday, July 27, 1972. He was accused of four counts of conspiracy to interrupt visits of South African sporting teams to Britain: the Wilf Isaacs cricket tour in 1969, the Springbok rugby tour in 1969-70, and the Davis Cup tennis match at Bristol in 1969, and conspiring to cause to be cancelled the 1970 cricket tour of Britain. The language of the charges was antique and verbose and to each of them Hain replied in a quiet voice: not guilty.

Although the charges had been brought on a private prosecution by a barrister, Francis Bennion, Hain was charged in the name of the Queen, a reminder of the medieval days when all prosecutions were private.

A panel of 24 jurors came into court from which 12 were to be selected. Who they were no-one but themselves knew. As the first 12 stepped into the jury box only one was challenged by the defence. Mr Brian Capstick, the junior counsel, called out the word "challenge" to a man whose appearance, in dress and facial characteristics, was that of a man of slight education and little worldliness. The defence was apprehensive about the nature of the jury due to try such a sensitive case but had nothing to go on save the names and occupations and appearances of the men and women who stepped into the box at the answer of their names.

Some of the selection was done for them by the obligation of Judge Bernard Gillis, QC, to point out to jurors that this was likely to be a lengthy trial — four to five weeks — and thus any person running a one-man business, or due to take their annual holiday in this period, would be well advised now to indicate this. Seven in fact took advantage of this escape route, saying their businesses would be spoiled or that they had booked a holiday which would be expensive to cancel. Small businessmen are usually opposed to the principles Hain and his colleagues stand for, so the defence was much relieved to have these weeded out for them. The final composition of the jury was nine white men, one white woman, one black Guyanese man, one Asian man,

The Judge then explained to the jurors the nature of the case and warned that if any of them were employed by, or on the committees of, any of the rugby, cricket and tennis organisations involved they should step down. "Also, if your view on matters concerning the racialist policies of apartheid, or on sporting matters, are such that you would feel you could not without bias or prejudice approach the matters about to be placed before you with a free, open and wholly righteous mind, then you should ask to be released," said the Judge. "You are not expected to come into the jury box without any knowledge of the world in which you live. But if your interest or prejudice is such that you cannot approach the matter with a wholly free, open and balanced mind, then you should seek to be released." The twelve members of the jury remained silent.

CHAPTER II

Above the Law?

Owen Stable, QC, who had two barristers assisting him, then outlined the case for the prosecution. Two rows behind Stable sat Francis Bennion and his solicitor. Hain's family and friends sat in the public seats.

As this was essentially a case likely to be decided on argument and political conviction, rather than factual detail, the strategy of the advocates was all-important. Stable's attack outlined the philosophy of Bennion and his organisation, Freedom under the Law, Ltd. This account of Stable's opening speech is of course edited, mainly to remove points which will be adequately dealt with later in the trial report. A counsel's preview of the facts is, after all, invalid unless witnesses later corroborate it with their own first-person, factual accounts.

Stable remarked that in his view juries were often not told enough at the beginning of a case what was their function. Explaining this and outlining the evidence took him the next day and a half. "Possibly from having had the indictment read to you you may recall that you have seen something of the facts that lie behind this case on TV and read about the events with which you will be concerned in newspapers," he said. "I would ask you to put that out of your minds. Your oath requires you to return a verdict in accordance with evidence you hear and read in this court.

"You are probably not going to have much difficulty in deciding what happened and you will see later why I say that. Such difficulties as exist in this case arise out of questions of law involved. This is where the judge comes in and has an all-important role to play in this trial . . .

"In each count Hain is accused of conspiracy. Conspiracy involves making an agreement. None of us goes through a day in our lives without making dozens of agreements. Each time you get on a bus you make an agreement with the transport board. The agreement is that you will pay the fare and the board by its agents will carry you. You cannot make a purchase in a shop without making an agreement. The agreement is that the shop will sell you what it is that you want to buy and you will pay the price. None of our normal business usually brings us to the criminal court.

"There are two kinds of agreement which constitute conspiracy. The first kind, where two or more people agree to commit a criminal offence. If people agree to commit a criminal offence something may intervene to prevent them from carrying out their agreement. If it can be established that the agreement was entered into, those entering into it are guilty of conspiracy even though the offence itself was not carried out. Perhaps the most famous conspiracy of this kind was the gunpowder plot, when a collection of men plotted and planned to blow up the Houses of Parliament. The fact that Parliament was not blown up didn't prevent those involved from being found guilty. Perhaps it is not irrelevant to point out that all those involved in the plot were not just thugs. Guy Fawkes himself was a devoted if misguided Roman Catholic who viewed the establishment of the Protestant religion in this country with abhorrence.

"The other type of conspiracy is where an agreement to do something not in itself criminal is made, but the agreement to try to achieve the ends is by unlawful means. One thing that may have struck you already from what I have said is that it takes two or more people to make an agreement, and if an agreement of a particular kind must be established to establish the offence of conspiracy it follows that it takes at least two people to make a conspiracy. Yet there is only one person in the dock.

"It is true that it takes two or more to make a conspiracy. You cannot conspire by yourself. And one of the elements which the Crown in this case will have to establish in respect of each of these four counts is that Hain was acting in conjunction with other people. The prosecution in this case must satisfy you that there were others involved besides Hain, but we do not have to establish who those persons were. One distinguished judge has said that the prosecution ought not to include the name of anyone in the indictment unless that person is charged with the offence if that person is available to be charged and available to stand trial.

"In this case the prosecution believes that the evidence which we can call before you establishes that Hain was guilty of each of these conspiracies. We can show that a number of others were also involved, and worked with him, but we do not have to, and do not propose to, establish who those persons were, although inevitably some names of others will probably get mentioned in the course of the case.

"The reason why the prosecution believes it can establish the guilt of Hain but is not seeking to establish who his confederates were, is that Hain wrote a book in which he set out a large number of facts which the prosecution has to establish to convince you of his guilt. Now where evidence takes the form of a written statement of fact the writing is only evidence against the author of the writing. By our rules of evidence what is written in the book is not evidence against any of the people whom Hain mentions as having helped him or planned with him or done things with him, but it is evidence as against him as the author. And reducing this rule of evidence to its simplest terms: if I say in a voluntarily written statement, 'Last Friday I and Potter [junior counsel] stole such and such a motor car,' the statement may be used by the prosecution as evidence that I stole the car but may not be used as evidence tending to show that Potter stole the car. If he and I were both on trial for theft the judge would have to tell the jury that they could not use my statement when considering the case against Potter. You will not think that any injustice has been done to Hain by being the only person put on trial when there were others involved as well as himself.

"It is a valid criticism of our system that the various rules which the prosecution must observe, which are designed to ensure that no innocent man is convicted of a crime, operate so that sometimes when a crime has been committed the small fry find themselves in the court but the big fish get away with it.

"By the end of the case you will be driven to the conclusion that Hain was at the very centre of these conspiracies, that there was no one else who played a larger part than he did, and that each of these conspiracies was planned and organised from his own home. I submit that he can have no valid complaint at having been put on trial, though there may be others who can consider themselves fortunate that they do not occupy the dock with him.

"Hain was the Chairman of the Stop the Seventies Tour Committee from about August 1969. The tour referred to in the title of the Committee was the tour of the South African cricket side which was planned for the summer of 1970 in this country. The actual STST Committee was formed in August of 1969, although some things were done before that. In 1969 the cricket authorities in this country, the Cricket Council, invited the South African cricket authorities to send a touring side to the UK in 1970, in much the same way as the cricket authorities here invited the Australian cricket authorities to send the team which is at present over here and playing against England and various County sides this summer. To invite the South African authorities to send a side to play cricket in 1970 in this country was a perfectly lawful thing for the cricket authorities to do.

"The invitation was accepted, and the tour was due to start in May 1970. As its name implies, the committee of which Hain was chairman had as its prime object the stopping of that tour. As I see it, the object of the committee was a lawful if controversial one, and had it been carried out lawfully no one could have complained. There is no country in the world where greater scope is given to the individual or group of individuals to make their views felt, and no country in the world where the authorities are more sensitive to public opinion than in this country. In recent years we have seen two decisions altered as a result of protest of individuals. In neither case did the individuals or the bodies that formed sink to breaking the law.

"When it was proposed to build a third London airport at Stanstead there was massive protest in Essex and West Hertfordshire. None of them did anything that at any stage infringed the law, yet the protest was successful, the airport was not built there. But a commission was appointed which then said the best site was Cublington. When that happened there was a terrific protest from the inhabitants there. And again the protest was conducted within lawful limits and again the protest was successful in its object and the decision was taken finally to build on Foulness.

"Now instead of following the good example of the Stanstead objectors Hain took a very different line. It would appear that he regards the many lawful methods by which a group of persons may oppose the decision of others, and the many lawful methods by which a person may protest against the actions and decisions of others as ineffective. He would appear to hold the view that provided he thinks the object he seeks to achieve is a proper object, any methods he thinks likely to bring about that object may be used, regardless of the law to which he is subject. That is a terribly dangerous philosophy.

"In this country each one of us may do as he pleases provided he keeps within the law. That really is the whole basis of our freedom. The freedom of the individual is not absolute. It never has been, and chaos would result if it were. Individual freedom, which in fact is one of the most precious heritages that we have got, is dependent upon each individual recognising that he is at all times subject to the rule of law, and that he has no right under any circumstances to set himself above the law.

"Once that ceases to be honoured by the general consent of the people as a whole the days of freedom are numbered, and indeed parliamentary democracy as we know it is being threatened. We are seeing the truth of what I have just said worked out in all its terrible reality in Northern Ireland at the moment. Once you get people of extreme views trying to impose those views on others without heed to the limits which the law imposes on you you get a situation such as has developed in Northern Ireland. It is the failure of some to recognise that only if we observe the law and live under its rule can we continue to enjoy the freedom which we inherited from our forefathers. And that failure to observe the law lies at the heart of many of the problems with which our generation seems to be beset.

"The attempt by some to set themselves above the law is at the bottom of almost all our problems, and in the course of this case it will be shown that Hain and his friends tried to set themselves above the law and that is why we are all here today.

"Hain holds views, which are no doubt genuine views, about apartheid in South Africa. He believes that the laws of South Africa in relation to its coloured population should be and would be modified if South Africa was isolated from the rest of the world. He would prefer it if people in this country stopped inviting South Africans to take part in sporting events in this country. His views on apartheid are views which are widely, I suspect generally, held in this country. Whether preventing South Africans from playing games in this country would achieve any modification in the laws of South Africa is perhaps a more open question. Certainly some people hold the views that the campaign against South African sportsmen will be more likely to cause a closing of the ranks amongst white South Africans behind the present South African government and more likely to delay rather than promote modification in the South African government's policy towards its coloured population. Happily you will not have to decide which of these competing views is right. Because the rightness or wrongness of the views on this question are irrelevant to the questions before you which are whether the law was broken by Hain and those helping him or whether it wasn't.

"I am sure that there are people who hold either view with great sincerity and with deep feeling. Certainly you will not hear any attempt to impugn Hain's sincerity or his motives. I merely recognise that there are others who with equal sincerity and with equal integrity hold different views. We are not concerned with his motive or his sincerity or his depth of feeling. We are concerned with the means he employed to attempt to bring about his object.

"The more freedom a society allows its subjects in the way of expression of opinion the more diversified the views will be. In such a situation it is essential that those who wish to propound their views should have regard to the freedom of others to propound their views and to respect each other's rights. That can only be done by both sides recognising that it is the law which sets the limits they are entitled to go to, and beyond which they are not permitted to go. It is quite clear that it was Hain's judgement on apartheid that led him to set out to stop the 1970 cricket tour.

"Although his views are wholly irrelevant to the issues you are concerned with you will be concerned with the methods he employed. It will emerge that Hain has made a conscious study of the methods of protesting against lawful activities of others. He would appear to judge those methods solely by the yardstick: did they achieve their object? And not by the yardstick: does the law of England permit such methods here?

"As you probably know the 1970 tour was stopped. So the primary object of his committee was achieved. But it was not achieved without considerable planning and without utilizing methods and without threatening to use methods which went far beyond any methods permitted by the law of this country . . ."

Mr. Stable then outlined some of the evidence he was intending to put before the jury, adding: "I have a formal statement signed by Hain admitting that he is the author of the book. This formal admission which Hain has made will be put in evidence in due course. As Hain is the writer of the book you are entitled in a case brought against him to treat what is written in the book as evidence of the truth of the facts stated in the book. Before drawing your attention to certain passages in the book I would like to make some general observations about it.

"It purports to contain a factual account of all the methods used by which the tour in the summer of 1969 was hindered and disrupted. It purports to contain a factual account of all the methods used by which the David Cup match in July 1969 was hindered and disrupted. It purports to contain a factual account of all the methods used by which the South African rugby tour was hindered and disrupted. It purports to contain a factual account of all the methods used to bring about the cancellation of the 1970 South African cricket tour and the means it was proposed to use to hinder and disrupt that tour if it had not been cancelled.

"It discloses that the author himself was present at and taking part in a number of unlawful acts by which the object of the conspirators was hoped to be achieved. It discloses a wide variety of unlawful acts: digging up pitches, throwing flour bombs on courts, throwing tacks on courts, gumming up keyholes, taking and driving away the bus in which players were driven to Twickenham, besetting players wherever they went. 'Besetting' is perhaps a word we don't use a great deal, but it was used in an Act of Parliament and that is why we have used it in the indictment. It means following them about and generally making life very difficult if not impossible for them. Hounding them, is perhaps one of the best words to use to describe what was done.

"These methods were not merely unlawful in the sense of violating the private rights of the players, spectators and organisers of the games, they were unlawful in the sense of involving the commission of a wide variety of different crimes. The book describes that not only were unlawful means used, but that the unlawful means which were used were directly organised and plotted — and in one case actually rehearsed — under Hain's direction at his home. The book discloses that the writer of the book was the very organiser and that the central headquarters was his home."

Mr. Stable read many extracts from Hain's book, "Don't Play With Apartheid", but none was more crucial to his case, and Bennion's purpose in bringing it, than the words on page 200: 'STST's direct action tactics — invasions of the field and disruptions, sit-downs, and obstruction of coach journeys, etc. — came under heavy fire. All too often, the more critical refused to view the campaign against the background of sustained lobbying, petitioning and 'constitutional/normal/ peaceful' methods that characterized the twenty years of work in the campaign for non-racial cricket described earlier. It was the narrow and unprincipled attitudes of British sports authorities which necessitated the switch to militancy. The tactics of polite and reasonable persuasion simply had not worked. And it was clear, particularly with cricket and rugby, that they would never work. New tactics had to be employed.

'By attempting to stop the matches, we were accused of "infringing on people's lawful rights to watch cricket and rugby". This may have been true, and taken out of the context of the issue at stake, sounds plausible. The fact that people's "lawful rights" are just as often "infringed" by militant farmers driving tractors through towns, by industrial strikes and by disruptions of traffic by mothers demanding a zebra crossing, is conveniently forgotten. There comes a time when the existing order, general or specific, has to be challenged directly. There often comes a time when there is no alternative to direct action. The principal point about direct action in this campaign is that it cannot be considered in isolation from the issue on which we were campaigning: that is, racialism. The crying need to take a committed stand against racialism far outweighs the watching of a game of rugby or cricket. The tactics of gentle prodding, supported with such zeal by our opponents (from the MCC to Mr Vorster), were a prescription for impotence. We were not content to stand idly by any longer. We chose militancy. And it is because of this that we won.'

"That passage", said Stable, "is the clearest possible admission that what he is throwing over as unimportant (i.e. normal constitutional methods of getting your point of view over) he simply dismisses. And he says, 'we had no alternative to direct action. We chose militancy and because of this we won.' What he is really saying is that we rejected the lawful methods by which we are permitted to get our view over — we chose to disregard the law, we chose lawlessness, we chose unlawful methods, and it was because we did so that we won. And he is also saying really that he is to be the judge as to whether his cause is so good that he ought to be permitted to throw the law over. Perhaps at a later stage we might consider just where that would lead.

"I daresay all of you here have many matters that you hold very dear. We see many things going on no doubt in other parts of the world that arouse us, and you can take country after country and see things being done there that one doesn't like. But to say — however deeply you hold your views — that that gives you a licence simply to say that because I am extremely sincere about this I can simply tear the law up and ignore it, that is what he in my submission is saying in that passage.

"When I come to what was actually done I don't think you would quarrel with my definition of direct action. My definition is: the use of physical force to achieve an object without regard to the rights of other people or to the limitations imposed by the law . . ."

Stable recounted the events of 1969 and 1970 and pointed out that at a press conference at the White Swan, near Fleet Street, Hain had stated that the rugby tour 'will be severely disrupted'.

"You may like to know of a proviso of Section 7 of the Conspiracy and Protection of Property Act of 1875," said Mr. Stable. "That is a section which says: 'Every person who, with a view to compel any other person to abstain from doing or to do any act that such other person has a legal right to do or abstain from doing wrongfully or without legal authority, will be liable to a penalty.'

"So that if you do things with the object of stopping somebody else doing what he has got a perfect right to do, or if you do it with the object of making him do that which he has got a perfect right to abstain from doing, then you are guilty of an offence. Using insulting behaviour, causing willful damage to property, are criminal offences. We now have Section 7 which really makes hounding people (or following them about, watching and besetting, etc.) a criminal offence if it is done with a view to compel them to abstain from or to make them have to do something, etc.

"You will probably not need to be told by me that to play rugby in England on a ground at the invitation of the owner of that ground is perfectly lawful. Equally, to go to a rugby ground and buy a ticket for a game of rugby gives you a legal right to watch that match without being interfered with. Equally the authorities have a legal right to arrange matches and have them played and profit from them. It is partly, if not largely, out of the money made from tours that rugby and county cricket clubs keep going. The authorities not only have a legal right to profit from these games, but they are also legally entitled not to have their rights violated.

"When we come to the rugby tour you will learn of a large measure of violence and innumerable breaches of the peace. Even if Hain is able to convince you that the worst violence and the worst breaches of the peace were not intended by him or his organisation, my submission is that direct action methods which were unquestionably intended and unquestionably planned and in at least one instance rehearsed by Hain and his associates were unlawful from start to finish. The whole campaign from the moment plans were made until the rugby team took off from Heathrow at the end of the tour went far far far beyond the limits permitted by the law of England.

"You will hear the evidence of De Villiers, and have read to you the evidence of two other players. You will hear of appalling treatment they and the rest of the team had to endure thanks to Hain's fertile, trouble-making propensities. A great many of these humiliations are recorded with positive pride in Hain's book . . .

"On page 128 of his book there is a highly significant passage. It records the secretary of the STST Committee (Hugh Geach) announcing, 'we are going to hound them everywhere they go'. That is precisely what the law of England says you may not do, and I have read you the section which says you may not do it, and if you hound people to compel them to abstain from doing what they have a right to do — in this case to play, watch or organize a rugby football game — you commit a criminal offence. You will see that the hounding process started before players had got out of Heathrow upon arrival ...

"From the time of arrival to their departure the rugby players were subjected to a torrent of insults, to hounding in every form, they were beset everywhere they went, and in my submission at no moment of time were direct action tactics kept within the limits permitted by law. They were at all times miles outside those limits ...

"In relating what happened I shall concentrate on those outrages which I shall prove Hain himself was present and participating in. But the essence of conspiracy is plotting, planning, scheming — the agreement. If I satisfy you by the evidence that what was done at various places where players were was unlawful — and the judge will help you on this — and if I prove that what happened was part of a plan in each case, that it was organised and arranged and not spontaneous, and if I prove that Hain was part of the organisation which set these demonstrations up and the unlawful means employed were part of the direct action tactics he intended should be employed (and it is not a case of one thing being organised and another done in the heat of the moment) it doesn't matter in my submission whether Hain was present or absent when a particular unlawful act was committed.

"You can conspire to rob a bank without yourself attending the robbery. We already know a good deal about Hain's position at the heart of the organisation. The committee of which he was chairman started off with the cricket tour in mind, but took up disruption of the rugby tour soon after it was formed ...

"About barracking and chanting at football matches: people can go to watch a play, and if they don't like what they see they are perfectly at liberty to barrack and boo to their hearts' content. If they like what they see they can shout encouragement and clap and cheer. If they think someone should be sent off the pitch they can shout to the referee to send him off and nobody in their right mind would suggest that that was an unlawful or criminal thing to do. But if a body of people go to the theatre or to a football pitch not to see the play but to wreck the thing and make it impossible for the actors to act or go to a football ground to make it impossible for the players to play, that is an entirely different kind of thing.

"That was made perfectly clear a hundred years ago in the case of *Clifford*. What happened was that one of the managers of one of the London theatres raised the prices of seats and some of the people who had customarily gone to see his plays thought that he was charging too much, so instead of staying away a number of them clubbed together and it became perfectly obvious that the whole object of their clubbing together was to go to the theatre and make such a shindig when they got there that it was quite impossible for the play to take place. They were brought before the court and they said, this is a ridiculous accusation, because after all you can go to a theatre and you can clap if you like the play and boo if you don't — you can make as much noise as you like. We did absolutely nothing that we are not perfectly entitled to do. So what is everybody complaining for that we have committed a criminal offence?

"What the judge said is perhaps worth reading: 'As to the existence of a riot in the house no doubt can be entertained. It appears that for a good many nights there were riots and of such a nature as to put an end to entertainment. I cannot tell upon what grounds people conceive that they have a right at a theatre to make such a noise that others cannot hear what is going on on the stage. Theatres are not a necessity of life ... proprietors of a theatre have a right to manage their property in their own way and to set what price of admission they think right to their own advantage.'"

At the outset of the case the jurors had each been given a copy of "Don't Play With Apartheid" by the prosecution. "This is good for royalties," quipped Stable. At first the judge inclined to the view that it would be excellent for the jurors to take the book home with them to read but a little later changed his mind on this, saying he had now realised this action might cause them to discuss the case with other people. In the event, the jurors were able to read the book during the many times they were kept out of court during the intricate legal tussles between the lawyers.

It is a readable book, but after Stable had spent a whole day discussing parts of it and commenting thereon even the most ardent admirer of it as a piece of literature would find he had been put off by over-indulgence. The book was at the heart of the prosecution's case against Hain and therefore by the end of Stable's day-and-a-half long opening speech the jury had been well introduced to his view of it.

CHAPTER III

Playing Under Pressure

The first week of the case had been devoted entirely to legal arguments (3½ days) and the prosecution's opening speech (1½ days). The trial proper could said to have begun on the second Monday morning, a drizzling, muggy last day of July.

The entire defence team assembled at the Old Bailey an hour before the Court case was due to commence to hold a tactical conference in the consulting room next to the Silks' Robing Room. Present were Peter Hain and his parents, Michael Sherrard QC and Brian Capstick, defending counsel, Larry Grant, the legal officer of the National Council for Civil Liberties and his assistant Yvette Gibson. They met to discuss the handling of the case now that the judge had made clear how he saw the law relating to the charges and the way in which it was evident the prosecution would conduct its case.

At the close of the previous Friday's proceedings Hain told his lawyers he felt it would be better to defend himself. It was not a new thought: he had been discussing the idea with close associates for several months. But after the first week of the case he had become more than ever convinced that he would have to go it alone if he was to stand any chance of acquittal. There were two fundamental reasons for thinking this:

The first was that the Judge appeared to have no sympathy with any argument put forward by Sherrard. Time and again the defence objections were rejected when sometimes, at least, they appeared valid. The persistent rate of the objections quashed was too consistent to pass unnoticed. Mr. Sherrard and Judge Gillis were old adversaries — the former had the previous year, for instance, persuaded the judge to fine John Bloom £50,000 instead of sending him to prison for fraud connected with washing machines. This was — and still is — a controversial decision. Hain and his advisers felt — perhaps quite mistakenly but nevertheless sincerely — that Mr. Sherrard and Judge Gillis were at loggerheads.

Secondly, it was clear to Hain that the matters he wanted to have brought out in the trial — the moral and political issues — would be blocked if the ethics and practice of the English Bar were followed, as his counsel were of course obliged to do.

A third and vital reason was that Hain had decided, with virtually none of his advisers dissenting, that he would not go into the witness box. He would be too vulnerable to attack. But to say nothing to the jury would be self-condemnatory; yet while acting as his own advocate he could express his views.

Sherrard and Capstick strongly advised against Hain taking over his own defence. They told him that the judge would not allow him to depart from the evidence and would step unmercifully on 'opinions' being injected into the case. The problems of handling the defence witnesses might well prove beyond Hain, they argued, and a few mistakes would make his case look worse. They were also worried at the effect the announcement of their dismissal would have on the jury: they might sympathize with 'the underdog' or they might see him as an arrogant youngster. Sherrard and Capstick emphasized to Hain and his parents at that meeting that they could not stop Hain dismissing them but when he was before a court of law on conspiracy charges he could not rely on sincerity alone as his defence.

It was decided to carry on with the normal defence arrangements, but when the court resumed at 10.30 a.m. there was time for even further reflection because the judge decided to let the jury read Hain's book until noon. Sherrard had won at least one argument in asking that the jurors should be able to judge the book as a whole rather than from selections.

It was a pointer to the macabre nature of the trial that the very first witness for the prosecution attended on a summons — not a volunteer. Albert Radford, a photographer on the Oxford Mail, gave evidence about pictures he had taken on 7 July 1969 of the damage to the Parks Ground at Oxford and again two days later between Oxford University and the Wilf Isaacs teams. His photographs became trial exhibits.

Far from being dragged to the court, the next witness had paid his own air fare from South Africa to be able to give evidence. Wilfred Isaacs, a South African-born Jew, told the court he had played cricket in England during the 1930s at club level and then had conceived the dream of bringing his own team to England. For 18 years he had sponsored the cricket team bearing his name. "It consists of present and ex-internationalists and top young players who I think have got great potential and that may well some day represent their country," he told the court. When he first brought the side to England in 1963 no one had taken exception but things were different when they returned in 1969.

At the first match on the Carrerras Ground at Basildon, against the Essex County side, he found on arrival a lot of police present near the club house and around the field. Soon after play began, while he was sitting outside the players' changing room, watching his side bat, about ten or 15 people ran onto the field. Mostly young men, they went to the pitch waving banners and sat down, stopping the play. The banners said, 'Keep apartheid out of sport' and 'Stop the 70 Tour' and people nearby said the demonstrators were Young Liberals.

"The reaction was antagonism towards the people who had prevented the game," said Mr. Isaacs. "People shouted out, 'Let's play cricket' and 'Why don't you grow up'." When the director of Essex cricket club asked them to get off the pitch a couple did so but when the police arrived a few walked off immediately, others had to be carried away. "Certain of them were still scuffling at the back of the pavilion and the interruption took up about 20 minutes," said Mr. Isaacs.

In his account of the incident in his book, Hain claimed that Brian Taylor, the Essex captain, had ordered Keith Boyce, the West Indian bowler, to bowl directly at the protestors, but Boyce had refused. Taylor had contented himself with kicking demonstrators. Isaacs said he did not believe Taylor had given this order, nor had he seen him kick the protesters.

During the next day's play he was telephoned by Billy Griffiths, the MCC

Secretary, with the news that the Oxford ground had been dug up, but by the time they got there two days later repairs had been carried out. A trench had been dug across the square and 12 or 15 different wickets had been affected. When they arrived in the team bus for this game there were a fair number of demonstrators lining the streets outside the entrance to the ground and he was handed a leaflet. The race issue then came up for the first time:

Stable: Was your side in 1969 an all-white South African team? No black African, however good a player, is allowed to play in it?
Isaacs: I didn't hear your question.
Stable: It is said that no black African, however good a cricketer, is allowed to play in it. Is that accurate, or what restrictions are you under?
Isaacs: I am under no restrictions. As a parallel it would be Mr. Robbins' team or the Duke of Norfolk's in England. I am entitled to have whoever I wish in my side.
Stable: Would you be able to have a coloured person in your team?
Isaacs: I have never considered it. In the next team there will be an African.
Stable: What is the standard of your side?
Isaacs: The standard is very high.
Stable: Are there many persons of African descent in South Africa of the standard of your side?
Isaacs: No.

Isaacs then described what happened in their second match, at Oxford. Two people ran onto the ground and pulled the wickets out and ran off the field with them. Police seized the two and returned the wickets to the cricketers. Other demonstrators in the crowd shouted 'No Ball' when the bowler was delivering at the batsman and mirrors were used to try and dazzle the eye of the batsman.

"I walked round the periphery of the ground and was referred to as 'Fascist Scum' and spat on. During the last war I was a fighter pilot on Britain's side. Later whistles blew and about 60 people ran on to the ground and seated themselves on the wicket and made speeches.

Stable: Can you recall who they said they represented?
Isaacs: 'I represent the Communist Party.' 'I represent the Liberal Party.' 'I represent the Labour Party.' And the fourth person represented a union, which, if I recollect correctly, was the railway workers union or something of that description.

Eventually the police carried the demonstrators off, watched by some 200 in the audience and a host of press and TV cameras. "The day was a failure and play stopped early because there was a very upsetting atmosphere," continued Isaacs. "The Oxford players who were our hosts were very upset about the incident but the next two days of the game took place without incident." Later games at Birmingham, Dublin, Portsmouth, Roehampton and at the Oval were also interrupted.

Stable: Are you in favour of what is called racialism in sport?
Isaacs: I am very much against racialism in sport.

Stable: Are you aware that you ever stated publicly that the demonstrators were definitely paid?
Isaacs: Yes.
Stable: What is the basis of that?
Isaacs: I spoke to some demonstrators at the Oxford game. They told me they were being paid.
Stable: Did they say who by?
Isaacs: All sorts of organisations. Various parties, the Labour Party, the Liberal Party and they mentioned the BBC.

When asked how his tour of England received their invitations to play games, Mr. Isaacs said that they were all channelled through one person, Michael Melford of the Sunday Telegraph. Everyone who had played for the Isaacs eleven had in recent years represented South Africa.

When Sherrard rose to cross-examine Isaacs he went straight to the point of the witness' own involvement in the case, asking if he had not already come once to England to give evidence in the magistrates' court, had been cross-examined there, and so far as the defence was concerned he had not needed to return again as his evidence could have been read. Isaacs said he had been asked by the prosecution to come to the trial.

Sherrard: Let's see why this might be important, Mr. Isaacs, and see what your part in this really is. Did you see Francis Bennion in South Africa after the 1970 cricket tour was cancelled?
Isaacs: I did.
Sherrard: Did you see Mr. Bennion speaking or hear him speaking at meetings in South Africa under a banner proclaiming "Pain for Hain"?
Isaacs: I did not.
Sherrard: Mr. Isaacs, were you aware that Mr. Bennion was in South Africa collecting money to support his private prosecution of Mr. Hain?
Isaacs: Mr. Bennion was in South Africa. The idea was to collect money for Freedom under the Law.
Sherrard: Limited?
Isaacs: I don't know whether Limited or Unlimited.
Sherrard: There is a company on whose behalf Mr. Bennion is said to be prosecuting here. Did you contribute directly to the prosecution fund?
Isaacs: I did not.
Sherrard: Did you contribute indirectly by agreeing to pay your own fare to attend the magistrates' court?
Isaacs: I took advantage of coming to England at the time on holiday and on business.

Isaacs was replying to persistent questioning, saying he paid his own fare and expenses on both visits, when the prosecution objected, Judge Gillis asked Sherrard to clarify the relevance.

Sherrard: Mr. Isaacs, what I want to know is, that the real truth is, that this is a South African-inspired prosecution of Mr. Hain?

Judge: What do you mean by "South African-inspired Prosecution"?

Sherrard: That this prosecution has been inspired by South Africans who wish to sponsor racialism in sport.

Isaacs: In no way has this cause been fostered in South Africa for South Africa's cause at all. And I am here representing a private team in a private capacity and happen to be here at a time that is convenient to me. I visit London every year.

Sherrard: Did you say (to the press in South Africa) following a reference to Mr. Bennion collecting money that you urged public contribution and that it started with the South African Rugby Board, which both pressured for funds and whose office was the receiving tip until last year? Did you say that?

Isaacs: That is correct.

Sherrard: The Board also paid the air fares for those who went to England last year to testify in the cricket case against Mr. Hain?

Isaacs: That is incorrect because nobody paid my fare.

Sherrard: The money has been collected in the name of the Peter Hain Prosecution Fund?

Isaacs: Correct.

Sherrard: You say that a non-white will play for your team. That would be good. Are you telling us that you are now allowed to include as a player in your team any African, Asian or person of mixed race?

Isaacs: I would like to clarify the position. Whilst I was in England I was referred to as a racialist. I am of the Jewish faith. The faith doesn't consider racialism in any manner and what worried me more than anything was that I pick the best sides I think in South Africa and although here you debar non-whites and Jews from your clubs I still love England, I still play against members of those clubs because I think I can do them justice. When I referred to bringing a non-white . . . I am not allowed to be a member of the London Sports Association . . . I thought, here is the opportunity to uplift their support in a demonstrative capacity because at a recent cricketing schoolboys week the standard was so low, it was about 3rd XI school standard. That if I could bring with me a non-white African that could learn and glean from the headquarters of cricket in England a tremendous amount, then I would be doing two things: I would be uplifting them from the standard of cricket and at the same time could get away from the reputation I have left in England.

Sherrard: I would rather you made that speech in South Africa and not here.

Judge: Counsel have plenty of opportunity to make comments at the proper time. There is no justification at this stage to be offensive.

Sherrard: Are you saying that you are now allowed to include as a player in your team any African, Asian or person of mixed race, that is someone who is actually going to be allowed to play cricket?

Isaacs: I am not saying that.

Judge: The Wilf Isaacs team is a private venture?

Isaacs: It is.

Judge: It is run by you as I understand it. Who apart from yourself is in charge of the conduct of its affairs? Have you got a committee?

Isaacs: I have two other people, a Mr. Roy Maclean, who plays for South Africa and has done a tremendous amount for young sportsmen in South Africa. And a Mr. Erikson who, when I was President of the South African Air Force Association, was President of the Naval Association. We have managed the affairs of the Isaacs XI together.

Judge: It is not government-controlled in any way?

Isaacs: It has nothing to do with the government in any manner whatsoever.

Sherrard: Mr. Isaacs, don't you think you ought to make it plain as to if you wanted to bring a team from South Africa comprising mixed races, you would have to have the permission of the Government to do so?

Isaacs: This position has never at any stage occurred.

Judge: You mean the government would have to authorise who should be in the team or do you mean that those people would need passports and other documents in the usual way?

Sherrard: All of those things. I am suggesting that you could not bring from South African a Wilf Isaacs touring team comprising white members, Asian members, Indian members, Africans, Chinese, travelling together to play together as a team. Would the government give you permission to do so? I think not.

Isaacs: I have never had at any stage to seek government permission for anything I have done in regard to the Isaacs XI and I could not tell you here and now what the position would be if an Asian, Chinese or anybody else were to be included in my team because I have not had to seek that permission.

Sherrard: Have you ever sought, as an anti-racialist, to include in your team, travelling abroad, during all these years, a single non-white player?

Isaacs: I have not.

Mr. Isaacs' equivocal attitudes on race came up again later in the cross-examination when he agreed that England Test players had appeared in his teams but none of them had ever been coloured. He sought to amplify this. "Mr. Basil D'Oliveira asked if he could play in my team when I was in England if it were permitted. He was very keen to wear the Wilf Isaacs' tie but he phoned me at Southampton to tell me that his services were required by Worcester and he would not be in any position to play for my side, to qualify for that tie." Asked by Mr. Stable if D'Oliveira had been free to play what would have been the attitude of himself and his team.

Mr. Isaacs replied: "He would have been quite free to operate."

Next into the witness box was Dawe de Villiers, who was captain of the South African rugby team which toured Britain between November, 1969 and January, 1970. By now the trial had moved to the Lord Chief Justice's court at the Royal Courts of Justice in the Strand as, during August, the Old Bailey was undergoing renovations. De Villiers told the jury of his experiences in England that winter. It was the first full account of what it had been like to be on the receiving end of a persistent direct action campaign.

"As soon as we left the airport building at Heathrow we noticed a number of demonstrators with placards shouting slogans as we walked out to get into the

bus. I remember one or two slogans, but I want to state that on the whole tour
we had demonstrators shouting slogans at us at games, at our hotels. Some of
them I remember very vividly but not which were shouted at the different
occasions.

"But on this occasion I remember two: 'Go home, go home Springboks' and
'racist fascists'. The demonstrators had placards with them. I can't really recall
what they said, they had placards right through the tour. From the beginning
even before we left Johannesburg we encouraged the players not to take any notice
of the demonstrators, because by taking notice we would fail in our aim to play
rugby. We thought we had to get them out of our minds. This was the first real
encounter with demonstrations and I think we felt a bit uneasy and a bit unnerved
when we went out and had all these people shouting at us . . .

"On the following morning at our first training session at Richmond, having
changed and started loosening-up exercises on the field, a few demonstrators
appeared with placards and came onto the field where we were doing our
exercises. We tried not to take notice of them as this was our policy right through
the tour. We got to concentrate on the game and try to get players to concentrate
on what they are doing. But a few of them came right up to where we were doing
our exercises . . . They were then taken off the field by a groundsman and, I
think, a policeman.

"On the same evening we attended a reception given by the South African
Ambassador to the U.K. We arrived by bus and there were quite a number of
demonstrators present with placards shouting slogans at us as we entered the
building. I can't recall any of the slogans they greeted us with, but after the
function, when we were about to leave, the police came in and told us we would
have to wait a bit because they wanted to clear a passage to the bus, and we had
to wait in the foyer for approximately 15 minutes. This was a bit unnerving. We
didn't know what the demonstrators were up to. But when we left the building
through a corridor to the bus I don't remember any of the placards, but one
particular slogan shouted at us I remember very vividly because it is very rude in
my own language. And some of the demonstrators tried to spit on the players.
One came up to the window where I was sitting and spat on the window next
to where I was sitting in the bus."

At this Sherrard objected. "Although, of course, the matter of spitting is extremely unpleasant — nobody would approve of it — it is by comparison with the
matters with which we are concerned possibly not the most serious," he said.
"What is very much more important is that it does illustrate the danger of the
prosecution seeking to allege that any act by any person, as a demonstrator,
whoever they might be, at any stage in this affair, is to be laid at the door of
Hain. Although in this particular case nobody alleged that because a demonstrator
spat at a player — nowhere is it alleged that he conspired to do it. I would ask
you to ensure that the prosecution does keep the matter within the confines of
what is already in my submission an enormously wide indictment," added
Sherrard.

Stable replied that it was perfectly true that in the particulars that had been given spitting at the South African rugby team was not specifically alleged, "In my submission it is all part of the story of the behaviour that de Villiers and his team were subjected to. It goes towards assisting the jury if he is allowed to tell his story as to what happened when later they do form a view as to whether what was done towards them was all part of a planned campaign or not."

Judge: Is it mentioned in any passage in the book on which you rely?
Stable: No. But in my submission it does go to that part of the indictment which alleges that the team was insulted and annoyed and that they were beset from the moment they arrived to the moment they left.
Judge: In paragraph 4 [particulars in the indictment of insulting and annoyance] you set out the matters: abusive and insulting shouts and slogans. I don't think that, apart from introducing the matter, you should go into any further particularity, because then the defence would be entitled to have some notice and be instructed.

De Villiers said that one slogan was shouted in Afrikaans, therefore he remembered it very well, and it was very rude. Roughly it was calling one's mother a whore.

"Before we left South Africa we didn't exactly know whether our first game would be played at Oxford due to demonstrations. Shortly after we arrived we heard that the game wasn't to be played at Oxford, but they still maintained that the game was going to be played somewhere else, and they asked us to prepare as if the game was going to take place. They kept the place a secret. We moved down to the vicinity of Bournemouth a day or two before the game and we had this preparation, because any sportsman would realise that the most important thing of participating in first-class sport was the mental approach — the psychological approach — and we had to get the players to concentrate on the game although we didn't know if it was going to take place. Only the morning before the game, round about breakfast, the players were notified that the game was going to be at Twickenham.

"The psychological approach to the game is of vital importance. Concentration is particularly built up in prior practice and team talks. And we had the team, as usual, preparing for the game, but it was quite difficult to concentrate on a game that you didn't know whether it was going to be played. And the unnerving effect the demonstrators had on us already — we tried to create the impression that it was normal, but it wasn't normal.

"We left Bournemouth early in the morning after breakfast by bus and had a picnic lunch on the way and arrived at Twickenham a few hours before the game. The field was empty with only police around. We stayed in the dressing rooms up to the time we had to get ready to go onto the field. Arriving at the field at the right time is part of psychological preparation. You go out to the field and you go out to play the game. Sitting around in the dressing room is not at all promoting or helping the concentration of the players.

"The first thing I noticed when we got onto the pitch to play was that there weren't many people in the ground. That was hardly surprising, because the ground to be used had to be kept secret and there had been a switch from Oxford. Slogans were shouted all through the game. I can't remember any slogans particularly. I remember at that time and in many other games they combined in shouting slogans like 'go home', 'Springboks go home' and the like. And that game was an example of what we experienced many times which was demonstrators trying to encroach on the field shouting slogans at us all through the game.

"Again we tried not to take notice of spectators. We thought that as long as we can keep players' minds on the game we will have the result of them concentrating and playing better rugby, so I don't particularly remember all the details of how spectators were placed. But there were three empty stands. A number of demonstrators got onto the field of play during play. Usually they tried to avoid policemen and get onto the pitch. Normally they tried to interrupt the game by sitting down. By sitting down they had to be removed by force from the pitch before the game could continue.

"The game was played under constant chanting of slogans and right through the game demonstrators tried to encroach on the field. What was quite true was that we were completely unnerved, this being our first experience of playing with demonstrators all around the field. You get used to noise on the rugby field — but I think particularly we realized this was not a normal crowd.

"For the second game at Leicester the rugby officials took great pains trying to get us to the ground avoiding demonstrators. There were demonstrators inside the ground, but not as many as at Twickenham, although quite a few managed to get onto the pitch. I think it interrupted play.

"Again, for the third match, at Newport, we had to get to the ground long before we normally would. We went to the ground by bus well in advance of the game and we drove into the ground, parked in front of the dressing rooms and we had to sit in the bus or in the dressing rooms — most of us stayed in the bus — for quite a large time which was again an unusual way of approaching the game. The precautions we had to take added to the effect of the demonstrators and it was unnerving to the players. At Newport it was a normal situation; shouting, a number of them trying to encroach on the pitch. Nothing out of the normal.

"On the night before the Swansea game there were a number of demonstrators outside the Dragon Hotel who were quite noisy right through the night, shouting whatever they did, making speeches. We had our normal team talk on the Friday night and in the rooms one could hear the noise coming from the street. The players found difficulty to sleep I think almost all night. I remember a demonstration especially the afternoon at the game. Precautions were again taken to get us to the field of play by slipping out of the back door of the hotel and being driven to the field in cars and we entered the field at one of the side gates. Getting out of the cars a number of demonstrators walked past and shouted slogans. A large contingent of demonstrators were behind the gate where they expected us to enter. We listened to them shouting and making a noise outside. It was definitely not encouragement — things like 'go home', 'fascist', 'racist', 'sieg heil' — that would be the type of slogans. There was one interruption which lasted quite some time, when a great number of demonstrators came onto the ground and ran to get to the middle of the field where they sat down and were holding onto each other and they had to be removed by force. Some of them were stopped before they got to the middle. Those who got through took hold of each other to try and make it difficult to be removed. The interruption lasted approximately 10 minutes. The important thing that a stoppage of that kind is in regard to the net effect on the game is that it interrupts the rhythm of the game, breaks concentration. And on that particular occasion after a few moments I remember picking up the ball and telling the players to try and move it around so that they could try and concentrate and try to stay warm. A policeman was injured and one or two players went to visit him in hospital the next day."

De Villiers said that the second Twickenham game on 22 November with London Counties stood out in his memory as what they thought was an important turning point on the tour. For the first time they managed to play the rugby they expected to play. "But I would say it was the normal — what had become normality — shouting of demonstrators were there as well. We had the blowing of whistles at most of the games, trying, I would imagine, to let the players think it was the referee's whistle and stop playing.

"There was a big demo at the Manchester game. A number of people were arrested, so we read in the papers. I didn't witness it.

"We had been hounded at all the games and we thought it was so important for the third Twickenham game to get a good night's rest and have peace of mind that we took the players and reserves to a hotel near Twickenham, because we were afraid that the same things would happen on the night before as almost any other games and to rest the minds of those playing. We left players not either playing or reserves back at the London hotel so that for the night before the Twickenham game some were in that hotel and others stayed in London. We slipped away late in the afternoon. The London hotel was the Park Lane in Picaddilly. I stayed at the hotel near Twickenham. So I only heard about the goings on at the Park Lane when other team members came out to Twickenham the next day. We were met as we came out as usual with slogans of the sort there were right through the tour, and demonstrators trying to encroach on the field and police around the field. One of the players said, 'look, a demonstrator has chained himself to one of the uprights'. It was during the match.

"We all had the impression that the England game, more or less halfway through the tour, was a turning point in the approach of the demonstrators, because up to that day they held demonstrations more at the field of play or a march or a number of demonstrators outside the hotel. But since Christmas and after Christmas we had the feeling the demonstrators were concentrating on the players — at the hotels, phone calls, following them around, etc. We had the feeling that they were trying to work on the nerves of the players instead of just demonstrating at the field of play. We had demonstrators outside the hotel in Bristol almost during the entire stay. One night I was awakened by the fire alarm. I went out and saw a number of players in the corridor and I thought demonstrators might have put the alarm off so I went back to bed. But I learned the next day that it was a smoke bomb and when that didn't go off the demonstrator tried to awaken the players by putting the fire alarm on. At Exeter quite a number of the players received telephone calls. I particularly received a call warning me that if we didn't go back to South Africa immediately something terrible was going to happen.

"In the Bristol game, 3 December, a man ran onto the pitch and scattered drawing pins all over the place. After he was removed players from both sides, referees, etc., looked all over the place to find them. A drawing pin would not have been a nice experience. I wasn't playing that match.

"At Gosforth against Northern Counties 2 January, a demonstrator managed to get on top of the cross bar and it was difficult to get him off there. There were two big demonstrations at Coventry, one Friday night. Repeated the next day. Quite a large number of demonstrators marched past the hotel with placards. On the way to Ireland, after we went through Customs, we were delayed a considerable time because of a bomb scare. We were called back and all our luggage was re-opened, and investigated.

"Before the Welsh international on 24 January at Cardiff Arms Park I remember a big demonstration in the morning, but the game was quiet. On return from there to London, arriving at our hotel, we had to wait quite a considerable time in the foyer because of another bomb scare and all the rooms were searched.

"In our last match at Twickenham, against the Barbarians on 31 January, apart from normal procedures, for the first time we encountered smoke bombs. They threw some things onto the field and orange and grey smoke came from them. Running through it wasn't a very comfortable experience. It felt a burning, and inhaling it was uncomfortable. It gave a slight burning in the chest like any smoke would do, I presume. Some things were thrown at us. I remember an orange.

"We tried right through the tour to work on the concentration and psychological approach to the game of the players, and under those circumstances to try and play good rugby. Although we realized this was almost impossible we nevertheless continued as far as the players were concerned to encourage them that psychologically we would get over the demonstrations. We lost three games out of the first five and we tried to say, 'well, we will get used to the demonstrations'. Another thing, it would be very unfair to our hosts to find excuses for losing games. Also it would have been very encouraging to the demonstrators to see they were having an effect on us. We tried, in speaking to the press, to say that it wasn't having an effect. But looking back on it it did. We reported it to the South African Rugby Board."

Cross-examined by Brian Capstick, junior defence counsel, de Villiers gave his reasons why he had not replied to a letter from the STST campaign asking him and members of his team to declare themselves against racialism in sport. "We were unanimous that we came over here to play rugby and though in the team we had players of different political opinions we decided that we came over here as a team and that we go on touring the country as a rugby team and therefore no player replied to this letter irrespective of his political viewpoint."

Within a few days of his giving evidence in the case de Villiers was back in South Africa. It was then announced that he would be standing as a Parliamentary candidate for the Nationalist Party — the proponents of apartheid — and it is fair to assume that this announcement had been delayed until after de Villiers had given evidence against Hain. It would have been a strong card in the hand of the cross-examiner if he had known. Later I asked Francis Bennison if he had known of de Villiers intention to join Vorster's party and he replied that he had "been surprised".

CHAPTER IV

Tennis Interlude

It was at this stage of the trial that the evidence of the interruption at the Davis Cup tennis match at Bristol in July, 1969 was touched upon.

At the time, to judge from the somewhat casual approach to this part of the evidence by the prosecution and defence alike, it did not seem to be what the trial was really about. It seemed at the time a charge thrown in to add weight to the 'scattergun' effect of the charges involving a multiplicity of actions by numerous people over the space of two years. From the manner in which the case was pressed, it was clear that the cancellation of the 1970 cricket tour was what it was mainly concerned with, the interference with the Isaacs cricket tour and the rugby tour being illustrations of the techniques of direct action used, and the prosecution witnesses — not unnaturally — were anxious to see some revenge for the annoyance they had been caused.

There were only three witnesses to the tennis incidents deemed necessary by the prosecution, presumably because Hain had described his involvement so explicitly in his book. The manager of the umpires described to the jury how three or four young people came from the stand onto the court during play in a match which featured a player from South Africa. The demonstrators were shouting and their presence stopped play. Members of the public were shouting out to them to get off, but about half a dozen policemen were needed to do this. The interruption to play lasted 10-15 minutes.

Two days later, said the witness, during a singles match, some flour bags came from the road outside the court behind one of the stands and about half a dozen landed on the court. Play was suspended because of the scattered flour and it was removed by a vacuum cleaner plugged into an electric point near the umpire's chair. The defence did not trouble to cross-examine this witness, and agreed that two other witnesses to the incidents need not attend court but could have their evidence to the magistrates' court read out to the jury. The referee and a linesman described similar incidents at the match, but none spoke of seeing Hain at any time, whom apparently they did not know.

At one point in the trial Stable told the jury that Hain's book could have been subtitled, 'How I Did It'. This was certainly true of the events at the Davis Cup match so far as they related to his going onto the court.

On page 119 of the book, Hain had written (and on this Stable relied):

"Early on the morning of the first day, Helen Tovey, Maree Pocklington and I set out to drive down to Bristol from London. The three of us, members of Putney Young Liberals, went with the vague intention of interrupting the game by sitting on the court. We were inexperienced, undecided about tactics, and rather apprehensive. We linked up with Mike Williams, another Young Liberal, at Bristol.

Police security was again tight, but we managed to buy tickets and nervously took up our seats, pretending not to know each other and trying to appear like ordinary spectators.

"In between sets we positioned ourselves at different points in the stands and, when the players were changing sides, jumped on to the court, unfurling our paper posters and displaying them to the crowd. We also called on spectators to join us and Maree tried to give leaflets to some rather unreceptive officials and players!

"After a few minutes, a leading official apologetically asked us to leave. I told him that I was sorry, but we could not. This was the signal for the police to come on and we promptly sat down, only to be lifted up and carried off. As we left the court area, I remember giving an interview to a reporter who agilely kept pace with our carriers as I spoke to him over the arm of one of the constables.

"We were held for over three hours. Never having seen the inside of a police cell before, we were all rather nervous. But we left our mark: on the inside of the door of cell 2, Redlands Police Station, Bristol, is neatly scratched 'Young Liberals 17/7/69'!

"On the third day, two more demonstrators ran on to the court and disrupted play, and a march was organized outside the ground by the Bristol Anti-Apartheid group, supported by other organizations. While the march was passing by one of the surrounding walls, flour bombs were thrown over, causing an interruption of twenty minutes."

CHAPTER V

The Meaning of Direct Action

Hain was in the hands of the police again in November of 1969, as Police Constable Anthony Rogers, stationed at South Norwood, London, described to the court. P.C. Rogers told how, at the match between the Springboks and Oxford University at Twickenham, the spectators started to climb the railings and come onto the pitch. He got hold of one man — he happened to be Hain but he did not know it at the time — who resisted him and tried to get onto the pitch. "There was a struggle and we both fell onto the floor." Some colleagues helped him grab hold of Hain and "we evicted him from the football ground. He was lifted bodily to prevent any further struggle and carried along the benches to the tunnel in the centre of the west wing and out, where he was taken to the police station", said Rogers. "He still struggled for a while. When we got to the tunnel he relaxed and he was then released and I took him to the temporary police station." Although scores of people had jumped over the railings at that moment, the press succeeded in getting a photograph of Hain actually being seized, and this was a trial exhibit. In cross-examination P.C. Rogers agreed that Hain had not been arrested or charged with any offence.

Seventeen days later, at the Springboks and London Counties match, again at Twickenham, Hain was in the hands of the police once more. P.C. Edward Myers, of Harlesden, told the court that the police were nearly shoulder to shoulder inside the railings when there was "one big rush, everybody at the same time and trying to get over in one place. I noticed a gentleman I know now as Mr. Peter Hain, wearing a sort of combat jacket and a pair of jeans, getting over the railings. As soon as he got over I restrained him and stopped him going any further. He did not offer much resistance — just moved his arms and legs. He went limp and we had to carry him off. He declined to give his name and said he would give it to a senior officer. He was taken to a temporary police room inside the ground. The sergeant recognised him and said, 'This is Mr. Peter Hain'. No charges were preferred."

The Rugby Football Union had appointed Stanley Couchman, a company director, of Esher, Surrey, to be its liaison officer with the South African team for the tour, and he described the various demonstrations already outlined by de Villiers, but his particular contribution to the prosecution case concerned the incidents at the Park Lane Hotel, where the non-playing part of the team were staying before the big international match in December at Twickenham. In order to get a good night's sleep, those selected to play secretly moved to the Excelsior Hotel at London Airport and the non-players stayed behind as a blind. During the night before the match, Bostick adhesive was poured into some of the hotel room locks in an attempt to stop them getting out and there were demonstrations constantly outside the hotel.

Mr. Couchman described how he was waiting in the lounge of the hotel when the coach driver of the team bus came in and said he had received a message that he was wanted. This was incorrect so he and the driver walked out of the hotel to go back to the bus and saw it moving down towards Piccadilly very erratically. "As I came out it veered over to the right of Piccadilly and then sharply back and finished up on the pavement just by the Naval and Military Club. It had struck a road engineer's van. I found the driver was sitting in the driving seat chained to the wheel so that he could not be pulled out. The coach was half full of players and officials. The police released the driver with a pair of cutters they borrowed from the contractors on the side of the road. The passengers were very badly shaken up and there was quite a big gathering around the bus. Even after the man was removed from the driving wheel demonstrators persisted in trying to stop the bus getting away, but it did so with the help of the police."

After recounting all the incidents at games and hotels up and down the country, Couchman said: "It eventually had its effect on the team. They became very strained, particularly the young members of the team. They maintained a very high standard of discipline but it was easy to see that in the long term it was having an effect. I have done the same job for the Australians and the All Blacks and this was quite exceptional. The situation was worrying and unparalleled."

In his book Hain had described the incident thus:

"Press reports of the action at the team's hotel were very confused. In the middle of the morning, one of the group, Michael Deeney, emerged from the Park Lane Hotel, impeccably dressed in a suit. He walked across to the team's coach which was waiting at the kerbside and told the driver that there had been a change of plan and that he was wanted inside. The driver responded immediately and went into the hotel, leaving the engine running. Michael promptly took his place and chained himself to the steering wheel as planned. At first, the coach occupants who included a number of the players, were just curious. Then they became a little restive. And this turned to positive fright when, apparently unable to resist the temptation, he drove the coach away. Michael's driving skills while chained to the wheel did not match his other skills, however, and the coach slowed into the back of a Post Office van parked about 100 yards up the road. By this time, the coach occupants had aggressively pounced on him. In the ensuing *melee,* a Springbok player broke Michael's jaw and he later had to be taken to hospital. The policemen, who had quickly arrived on the scene, had a difficult time freeing him. The chain was made of hardened steel and they had to cut through the chain lock with cutters appropriated from a nearby roadworks gang. After this incident the coach was driven back to the hotel. But even then, when it finally departed for the match, it was delayed for some time by sit-down protesters."

Mr. Stable was later to contend that the words "chained himself to the steering wheel as planned" implied that Hain had a part in it.

CHAPTER VI

"Peaceful Invasion"

With the benefit of hindsight, it can be stated that the next witness was almost certainly the most crucial to the jury's ultimate view of the three charges concerning the rugby and cricket matters. Gordon Winter is a journalist specialising in writing about South African affairs from Britain. Born in Yorkshire, he spent some years in South Africa as a journalist but after giving evidence for the prosecution in a famous murder trial, the government deported him as 'undesirable'. With the arrival of South African teams in Britain and meeting such an unusual form of opposition, he was able to bring his talents as a photo-journalist into play. More than any journalist in London then (1969) he knew what it was all about; he knew the Hain family and their stormy background in South African politics, and he knew the impact the demonstrations would have in South Africa. When preparing his case against Hain, Francis Bennion asked him to make a statement to his solicitors about what he had seen of the demonstrations, but Winter refused. Like the first witness, he attended on a summons. He produced a number of photographs which were made trial exhibits.

After explaining where he had taken some of the photographs and what they depicted, Winter early on showed that he was not the usual prosecution witness. Answering a question from Stable about what happened at the Twickenham game on 22 November Winter replied: "It was just a peaceful invasion of the pitch. There was no violence. They went out of their way to be peaceful and offered no violence whatsoever. I managed to get behind the police lines by a bit of a ruse and I took photos from behind the police lines. I was facing the crowd and I was actually amongst the police when they dealt with certain people. At the Springboks match against Scotland on 6 December, there were incidents between demonstrators and policemen which I photographed. I think only one or two managed to get on to the pitch, because that was one of the hardest pitches to get onto. The police were incredibly well-organised, powerful and vicious."

Winter then produced photographs of smoke bombs on the field at the game against Barbarians at Twickenham on 31 January, 1970, of cushions being thrown at the demonstrators by people in the stands, and of a steward throwing a smoke bomb from the field back into the crowd. "It became a bit of a joke", he told the court. "Ping-pong fashion, as cushions were thrown to the demonstrators they threw cushions on, and they also threw oranges, tomatoes, smoke bombs. And the stewards also joined in the game and threw back oranges and smoke bombs."

Winter's main statement of evidence was quite brief, confined only to what the photographs depicted. His cross-examination and re-examination lasted several hours. Sherrard opened his interrogation by saying that he in no way wished to go behind what all journalists regard as confidential sources of their information, for which Winter thanked him, "because I am here under subpoena, most unwillingly, to give evidence for either side."

Sherrard pointed out that the day of the demonstration at the Oval against the Isaacs team, when people sprinkled stones on the pitch and trod them into the earth, was the same day as the Davis Cup demonstration at Bristol in which Hain admitted taking part. Winter replied: "I know for sure Hain was not at the Oval on that day, and to the best of my knowledge he had nothing to do with this particular demonstration."

This answer gave the defence the opening to exploit their main line of rebuttal to the charges: that Hain could not be held responsible for everyone's demonstrations against the South African teams as the elaborate conspiracy charges stated.

Sherrard: So far as this demonstration is concerned, are you in a position to tell us from what you heard said at the ground during the demonstration by people arguing politics on the wicket or making political speeches on the wicket — can you tell us what groups they represented, or individuals acting for themselves?
Winter: They were from groups, individuals acting for themselves. I followed the rugby tour, but the Wilf Isaacs demonstration was something of a mystery occurence. It was a very odd source from which I obtained my information.
Sherrard: What about the people on the pitch?
Winter: They were all unknown to me with the exception of one lady. She was from the Anti-Apartheid Movement.
Sherrard: Did any people on the pitch give any indication as to what groups they represented?
Winter: Yes. An attractive young lady called Christabel Gurney told me she was an Oxford Graduate, a teacher, and that she was from the Anti-Apartheid Movement. Tony Emerson said he was interested in Portugal. He was a computer programmer, age 24. Douglas Marchant, age 26, said he was interested in Swaziland, as I remember rightly. Graham Mitten said he was from the South Croydon Labour Party. Richard Chesham — I think this is the one who said he was from the GLC. I gathered there was some agreement between them before the match that they would do this.
Sherrard: You have told us that the demonstration at the Oval was a peaceful invasion of the pitch with no violence whatsoever, and that those that went onto the pitch went out of their way to be peaceful?
Winter: No question of that whatever.
Judge: What is a 'peaceful invasion'? No violence?
Winter: I am not saying that demonstrators never used anything like force . . . but when it was used, as they explained it to me, as in pushing through the police lines to get to the pitch, they called that direct action. They will push with the least possible violence to get through.
Judge: Is there a distinction between force and violence?
Winter: Yes, you have put it better than I have. Using force of the minutest possible strength. But it wasn't necessary at the Oval. Nobody stopped them.
Sherrard: Being the South African expert that you are . . .
Winter: I didn't say expert. Specialist.

Sherrard: In any event these matters would have had a particular interest for you?

Winter: Yes. I was writing a story on them for various papers.

Sherrard: I am right, am I not, that Hain always emphasised non-violence?

Winter: Very much so. In fact sometimes when I used stronger words than were necessary Hain made it clear that I wasn't to highlight any stress on the subject in interviewing him.

Sherrard: He didn't want any hint in the way the matter was put over that he was in favour of violence?

Winter: Oh yes, he made it very clear.

Sherrard: The same is true, is it not, of his disapproval of willful, malicious damage to property? Or didn't that arise?

Winter: From my conversations with Hain you are right. From my knowledge of my conversations with him, yes. But there is a thing I must add here. I don't know if Hain suggested or authorised or agreed to the use of smoke bombs being thrown onto the pitch, but if he did then they damage the pitch.

Sherrard: Dealing with his general attitude?

Winter: On that level you are right.

Sherrard: Were you one of the journalists who interviewed a number of people after there had been some daubing of some cricket ground buildings on 19 January?

Winter: I know nothing about that subject. It was cleaned up by the dailies and dead for me on Sunday. I saw Louis Eaks on several occasions but never about that.

Sherrard: You indicated that something you had said about one of the photographs wasn't wholly clear. I am asking you about that now. What do you want to make clear?

Winter: Yes. To be strictly fair the pictures handed in here of the Edinburgh match give slightly a one-sided picture. I took quite a lot of pictures at this match. I understand the prosecution have their own reasons for using these pictures, but there were other pictures which showed the other side of the coin [he produced a picture of police lunging at one demonstrator]. This sums up the point I would like to make. That all the other pictures show what might appear to be demonstrator-aggression, and that shows quite clearly police-aggression.

Judge: If you have any others with you which you think it is right one should look at in order to get the full and just view of what is revealed in the earlier photographs do please produce them now. I want you to keep out no photograph you have which you think it is essential or desirable one should look at in order to get a full and just view of what is revealed in the earlier photographs do please produce them now. I want you to keep out no photograph you have which you think it is essential or desirable one should look at in order to get a fair judgement.

Winter: I have 1,000 negatives. Obviously if you choose your photos you choose what you want. Some of my photos show quite clearly that as the tour progressed the police got more vicious and that caused a lot of trouble. This one shows quite a few policemen plucking a demonstrator out of the crowd. This is a crowd beneath them. The police are higher than the demonstrators. The police tactics was to pluck out one of the most vociferous. They would grab his testicles — this was common practice — and give them a good squeeze and give him a good hammering. The picture shows one policeman going for his testicles. This in turn enraged the

demonstrators and they became more aggressive. They spat at the police. It was
a progressive thing that led to unhappiness all round. In this match certainly
the police were to blame. No doubt about it. I was myself arrested, for taking
pictures of that incident. I was finally allowed to go when I proved I was not
from the underground press. I produced a National Union of Journalists card. Two
other journalists were assaulted at that match. Frank Herrman of the Sunday Times
was given a hard time by the police. He complained to me afterwards on the plane
back. I think all the press that were in my vicinity agreed that the police had been
diabolical.

Sherrard: Hain wasn't at Edinburgh?

Winter: Not physically. But he was there in spirit.

Sherrard: No doubt about that, but I am anxious to establish his physical absence.

Winter: He wasn't there, or if he was I didn't see him.

Sherrard: It is right, is it not, that there was protest which came from every cross-
section, every part of the community in relation to the rugby tour, the cricket
tour and so on?

Winter: Yes.

Sherrard: Isn't it right that there were protestors from political groups in the
House of Commons?

Winter: Oh, yes, at lunch in the House of Commons I even found that there were
Tories who supported Hain, personally, privately.

Sherrard: Members of the House of Lords who took a strong view?

Winter: I didn't talk to any. I don't know.

Sherrard: Bishops?

Winter: Yes, some of them definitely.

Sherrard: Local organisations up and down the country and the length and breadth
of the country? Acting on their own initiative?

Winter: Judging from what Hain had said in the papers, they worked out their own
policies, yes. No doubt about that.

Sherrard: Unions had formed committees?

Winter: Yes. To show solidarity with Hain's, with STST's aims and objectives.
When I say Hain it was because he was made a figurehead.

Sherrard: He says in his book he was really elected by the press. Is that a fair
statement?

Winter: Yes. I was there and I know what happened. It was absolutely true. The
whole thing took him completely by surprise. At the formation of the STST Committee which was held at the White Swan it was quite clear that knowing the
people involved, knowing the Hain family as I did, and their background, it was
clear that Eaks and Geach — I thought Eaks would certainly be the leader of the
STST campaign because he was the most outspoken chap — sometimes unwisely
outspoken. Then all of a sudden Peter was chosen because he is a very cool, articulate,
independent, reasonable man and it was like a bombshell. You phoned Peter and
you got what you wanted. He understood your terms of reference which many
people don't. It only takes about three or four phone calls from a pressman — there
were possibly about 15-20 people there representing different movements — and it
was possible to phone any one of them because we decided who we wanted to

talk to. And naturally when we chose a man like Peter, and he is articulate, he educated us too, because I at least didn't know much about the aims of STST then, he educated us and this is why, I think, the ball started rolling and Hain was elected by the press. That is the way he was elected, because he happened to be the most articulate for our purposes.

Sherrard: Of course, this would mean that whenever a statement was made, in relation to these tours, if it was made by Hain it would be reported to have been uttered by him and his photo would appear in the newspaper sometimes to go alongside that story, for the reasons you have said?

Winter: Yes. He was the clearest speaker. A dynamic young man. A new face. As simple as that.

Sherrard: You understand that it is suggested in this case that Hain conspired in what was said to be a nationwide conspiracy with people all over the country to commit all sorts of unlawful acts. Have you any doubt at all but that there was a very large element of spontaneous independent action by individuals acting on their own spontaneously by way of protest up and down the country?

Winter: Absolutely definitely no doubt about the fact that there were spontaneous protests.

Stable then exercised his right to re-examine the witness to clarify any points raised in the cross-examination.

Stable: Was STST a committee consisting of persons who themselves claimed to represent other organisations?

Winter: Yes. At the White Swan press conference they stated they were the representatives of those bodies.

Stable: Hain, in his book, refers to a number of them. As far as you could make out were the representatives there representatives of other groups and had they pledged their support for the committee and was a representative of the Anti-Apartheid Movement there?

Winter: Yes. Alan Brooks.

Stable: This formation of STST really was promoted, was it not, by Hain, Geach and Eaks? The Young Liberal Movement? It grew out of that?

Winter: That is what I gathered. I am not quite sure if I answered that correctly — could you rephrase the question?

Stable: Would I be right in thinking that STST consisted in a number of representatives of other organisations?

Winter: Yes.

Stable: And that the prize movers in getting it formed were the three Young Liberal representatives present at the press conference?

Winter: That is where I think I misunderstood you. I didn't hear the word 'prime mover' before. They were the more articulate, and so they led me to the opinion that they were prime movers.

Stable: Where Hain on page 121 of his book said: 'People who formed the nucleus of the committee early on were relatively inexperienced in national single-issue politics. Because of the initial resistance from those who were then more experienced than us and who would otherwise have seemed logical people to direct activities and take decisions, Hugh and I were put in the position where we had to take the initiative largely on our own.' Except that you would like Eaks' name included you would not disagree with that last statement of fact?

Winter: I will agree with that, on the level that they were put in a position where they had to take the initiative largely on their own, being the keen, young, energetic, articulate young men that they were. I would agree with it on that level, and I think that is what he meant.

Stable: Did you gather from the press conferences that their object was — by means of using direct-action tactics — to prevent the 1970 tour from taking place? But if they didn't prevent it from taking place then to demonstrate by direct action tactics against it?

Winter: Yes. They intended to do everything in their power to stop the South African cricket tour of Britain.

Stable: Was anything said at that first press conference about the rugby tour?

Winter: Yes. It was discussed at length.

Stable: Did they say they intended demonstrating against it by direct action tactics and organising demonstrations?

Winter: I gathered from the press conference that the spokesmen — or the people who said they were representatives of the bodies I have already named agreed to coordinate in activities to show their disapproval of the rugby team and that they would help each other and coordinate activities in making demonstrations against that team and its tour.

Stable: I gather from your evidence that you have had a number of conversations with Hain from time to time? We are told in the book that the headquarters of STST was Hain's home. Are you able to confirm that?

Winter: That is a very tricky question to answer. I would venture to say that in the same way that Hain was 'elected' by the press which was a rather strong way of saying we chose to phone him because he gave us the answers and the headlines we wanted by the same token — by the nature of our phone calls — his home was the prime target of newspapermen and thus became 'the headquarters of STST'.

Stable: I fully appreciate what you said about how he came to be chosen as chairman. He was less wild than some, articulate, and so on. But having been elected, thereafter on any document he signed himself as "Chairman of STST" did he not?

Winter: I don't remember. I certainly never used the term. I don't remember using that word. I think I always wrote "leader of" or "spokesman for". That was my version.

Stable: Were you present at the press conference when that cricket tour was cancelled, on 22 May?

Winter: Yes. I tagged it, "the victory conference".

Stable: Was that held at the White Swan?

Winter: Yes. The same place the press conference for the formation of STST was held. Because I understand it was very cheap.

Stable: Were the leaders of the agreement which you have just spoken about at the top table?

Winter: At the top table — Hain, Brooks, Jeff Crawford . . . But they weren't all present at the STST formation. Jeff Crawford came into it halfway through the act from his own West Indian Standing Conference. Hain was one of the persons at the formation.

Judge: Who presided at the victory conference?

Winter: Nobody presided. These things are very loose. Nobody stands up and says, 'I am the boss'.

Stable: You couldn't say which of those five was presiding?

Winter: As far as I know nobody ever presided. Hain, in any case, came late. Various people had made small utterances before he arrived. But they all did so in respect of their own movements and their own opinions. He came and was interviewed and photographed and said he was associated with STST.

CHAPTER VII

The Might of the Police Force

London's riot chief since 1968, John Gerrard, rarely appears in the witness box. As Deputy Assistant Commissioner in the Metropolitan Police he has many assistants who can carry out this part of the job while he concentrates on gathering information and devising strategy. Thus his appearance in this case was of particular interest. He described how at the very beginning of the Springbok rugby games there was a ratio of 1,000 demonstrators to 10,000 spectators. At a normal rugby game at this ground slightly less than 100 policemen would have been employed on crowd and traffic handling, but on this occasion it was thought necessary to use 540. Gerrard said that he went to Leicester with a contingent of Metropolitan police to give assistance to Leicester and West Rutland constabulary. There were repeated attempts to break various cordons.

For the Twickenham match on 22 November, he again would have used 100 policemen had things been normal but on this occasion he used 923. About 300 demonstrators who had marched from the station got in just before the kick off, making an estimated 2,000 demonstrators present inside. There was almost continuous shouting of slogans and a wire fence had been erected between the police cordon round the pitch and the crowd.

"The demonstrators got over it by making what you might call a human ramp whereby the ones behind would run over and get over the fence. Those who got over ran and sat down on the pitch during the game.

"Pennies, fruit, toilet rolls, tacks were thrown at the pitch during the game but because of the distance they fell in the intervening ground in the main. On two occasions in the second half people got onto the pitch and smoke bombs and fireworks were thrown. We ejected 189 persons and 50 were arrested. After the game, about 1,000 demonstrators had the usual march back to the railway station, but instead of ending there they went down to the police station and demonstrated, which made it necessary to clear the road."

At the international match on 20 December, there were about 2,000 demonstrators gathered at the railway station, with Hain accompanying them, said Gerrard. About 1,000 more demonstrators were inside. He had thought it necessary to employ 1,560 police to handle this game instead of the normal 4-500 for an international. Gerrard had no illusions about the volume of support the STST campaign had at games — at the 31 January game against Barbarians he estimated that 2,000 protesters marched from Twickenham railway station and between one and two thousand more were inside the ground. Just before the kick off about 20 packets of dye and a number of smoke pellets were thrown onto the ground. A short time after the start of the game there was a concerted but not successful attempt to get onto the pitch. A number of police officers were injured by having pepper thrown in their eyes. Forty-eight people were ejected from the ground and 23 arrested. He had used twelve times the normal number of police; if he had not they could not have kept public order.

Stable: On the last match you saw Hain yourself?

Gerrard: Yes. I saw him outside the gate in Whitton Road shortly after the kickoff.

Stable: Were you then aware that a number of demonstrators were in possession of packets of dye? And did you stop Hain?

Gerrard: I was. I did.

Stable: Did you ask him if he had any packets of dye?

Gerrard: I did. He said he didn't. As he was wearing an anorak I patted the outside of his anorak and his pockets to see if there was anything bulky in them. Being satisfied that he hadn't anything bulky, I expressed the hope that he wasn't going to obtain any such thing from his friends inside. To that he said, "you don't think I would be so silly as to tell you, do you?" I then indicated to the police constable who was checking people that he should let him through. I had two interviews with Hain at New Scotland Yard. I saw him in connection with the demonstration for the 20 December game. He came to see me first on 4 November. On my recollection he was alone, but may have had someone with him. It was an exploratory talk and he could well have been accompanied. And again on 3 December 1969. On that occasion he was accompanied by Alan Brooks of the Anti-Apartheid Movement and Ron Taylor of the Twickenham Branch of the Anti-Apartheid Movement.

He wrote to us first of all at the end of October asking if he could have a demonstration at the England game. That was why I had the first meeting. I told him to contact me again nearer the date of the match to make further arrangements and he did do this.

Stable: Did you at either of those meetings explain what you understand to be the limits to which one could go in organising a demonstration?

Gerrard: Yes, he told me what he wanted to do and I told him what I thought was reasonable, and I also pointed out the possibility of a counter-demonstration, and the necessity of keeping his demonstration under control. At the first meeting, the intention was to form up in Murray Park and march down Whitton Road and disperse. When we held the second meeting it was agreed that they would form up outside the railway station and then march to Murray Park for a meeting, after stopping at Whitton Road to hand in a petition.

Stable: So what he sought to do, and informed you he was arranging, was to simply form up at the railway station, go on to Whitton Road, hand in a petition and take his march on to Murray Park and hold an open air meeting there and then disperse? And if he had done that there wouldn't have been anything anybody could take objection to?

Gerrard: Right.

Stable: Was it clear that for what was being organised for this match the National Anti-Apartheid Movement, the Twickenham Branch of it, and Hain's organisation were all three acting together?

Gerrard: That is the impression I gained from the interview.

Judge: If you had known that he had what he did have in his pocket what steps would you have taken?

Gerrard: I would have arrested him.

Stable: Can you give me any indication of the cost of the special policing that was done for just the four matches at Twickenham.

Gerrard: The cost of arrangements for the four games in London was approximately £38,500. Approximately £34,000 would have arisen if police officers had been engaged on duty elsewhere. The additional cost, therefore, was in the region of £4,500 and this was recovered from the clubs in the form of special service agreements. So that there was no additional cost to the taxpayers, but these divisions were deprived of the normal services of their men.

Stable: So what you do in essence is really to deplete the divisions all around and bring the officers into the area of concentration and charge the organisations with those police officers who are not on duty at all?

Stable: Not as simple as that. The organisers of certain events pay for the services of officers on certain kinds of duty. It happened that this is how it worked out on that occasion but it could equally well not have worked out that way.

If the Stop the Seventy Tour demonstrations were the biggest and most bothersome to the London police, they were certainly not a rare phenomenon. Gerrard told the court that there were an average of 500 demonstrations a year in the capital and he had handled 1,000 since the STST campaigns. He agreed with Sherrard that the protests against the South African teams came from as wide a cross-section as one could reasonably imagine and a very large number of different organisations, unions and committees were concerned. On the 20 December game at Twickenham he recognised Lord Soper, the Bishop of Southwark, the Bishop of Woolwich, the Bishop of Stepney and the MPs Russell Kerr, Ann Kerr, Peter Jackson and Ian Mikardo.

Developing the line of "corporate action" as Hain's defence, Sherrard asked Gerrard: In relation to the 31 January game, you told us that you didn't discern any pre-arranged signal when people started to move onto the pitch?

Gerrard: No. They went at that time but whether they just followed each other or whether it was pre-arranged I don't know. I agree that it could equally be that somebody started it and others followed.

Asked by Sherrard if Hain was not a young man of perfectly good character, the Deputy Commissioner replied: "Well, he has got one conviction for wilful obstruction in relation to a demonstration."

Sherrard: But he is really a very nice young man of good character?

Gerrard: That is a matter of opinion.

CHAPTER VIII

"How a Demonstration Ticks"

Essentially this was a trial involving big names, powerful reputations, tough and diverse personalities. Publicly lawyers will tell you that it is what is said in the witness box which counts; privately they will tell you that it also matters a great deal who says it. One of the prosecution's big guns was Wilfrid Wooller, who told the court that he was a Master of Arts, a Justice of the Peace for Cardiff where he lived, Secretary of Cardiff Cricket Club and was for 14 years captain of the Glamorgan County cricket side. He was also a member of the Cricket Council, the national ruling body for the game. The defence took no exception to his statement of his educational qualifications nor to the fact that he was a magistrate.

Wooller was not asked by the prosecution what involvement he had with rugby — he is in fact a former Welsh international — but immediately asked him if he was present at Swansea when the Springbok rugby team played there. Wooller said a procession had gathered outside the Guildhall and was allowed by the Chief Constable to go past the rugby ground. In fact the march stopped on a bank almost beside the main stand. This was Wooller's description of the scene:

"There were a number of banners such as 'Boks Out', anti-racialist slogans. They were continually shouting at passersby heading for the match. There were some 17 to 18,000 coming to the game. They screamed 'Fascist swine', 'Racist pig'. Their behaviour was appalling. Four-letter words were hurled about. They didn't make any move against the police when they arrived beside the main stand. The stand at Swansea backs right onto the main road and the road and pavement come right up against it. Beside it is a bank which is part of the perimeter. It is quite wide at that point. There are some small gardens there that back onto the ground and most of the demonstrators climbed up onto the bank and stood hurling abuse at the passersby who were disgusted with what they were being subjected to. They attempted to break a cordon of police which formed shoulder to shoulder. The police were in a position directly between the demonstrators and a very large section of the crowd which was going in through the various entrances of the stand. The demonstrators tried to break the cordon but at this point I had gone into the ground and to a point at the back of the stand to the press telephones. The windows look straight down onto the site where the demonstrators were. I would be where this gallery is now and at about the same distance, looking down onto what was happening. They several times tried to break the cordon. They were using wooden sticks and palings from garden fences. At one stage the public behind the line of policemen had to go to their assistance, otherwise I think there would have been a very serious situation. Had it broken through into the crowd, and the crowd were getting somewhat bad-tempered by that time about the abuse that was being hurled at them, there would have been a serious situation had they broken that cordon. There were one or two people injured. The police appeared to be arresting one or two individuals who were hurling themselves at the police cordon. I saw an ambulance coming up towards the crowd but I couldn't see what was happening.

"A fair number of demonstrators had got into the ground and had been accumulating at the Mumbles Road end. Just to the left of the stand, and there were a number in the enclosure at the west end of the ground. They were shouting abuse such as 'Fascist swine'. They shouted abuse at both the visiting team and at the home team for playing them. There were a number of scuffles in the enclosure. One could see movement in the crowd where demonstrators had expressed themselves too forcibly. There were scuffles between spectators who objected to the demonstrators and with demonstrators. About 18,000 spectators attended the match and a very small proportion, about 100 or 120, were demonstrators, all collected together in one part of the ground.

"About ten minutes after half time groups of people burst from the left of the stand and from behind the goal posts and ran across the field towards the middle of it. It would have been, I suppose, about 50 people, but there was somewhat chaotic conditions because the rugby club had a number of officials around the ground who had volunteered to protect the game and they had been minding their own business around the boundary when these people broke loose. They straightaway went after them bringing them down with some splendid tackles by which time the police moved in and had to remove these people who lay on the ground and resisted movement by any way they could. They kicked and struggled to prevent being moved. They were lifted to the touchline by four or five people each and I would say in about five minutes the ground was clear. Play had been stopped for the whole time. The game then proceeded but the crowd were very angry indeed and I would say that had not the rugby stewards been around the crowd would have gone on and there would have been some very serious injuries. During play of the second half there were minor scuffles, minor fights in the corner."

Wooller also described lesser incidents at later Springbok games at Newport and Cardiff.

"I went early to Twickenham for the match against the Barbarians", he continued. "I wished to see the formation of the demonstration. I had now become interested in the phenomenon of demonstrations just to see what made a demonstration tick. I therefore went along to where they were meeting. I was in a good position because it formed up in a viaduct under the main road bridge. We could see the whole formation. We watched the banners. We could see the organisers, the car with the public address system at the front and so on. Peter Hain was at the head of the column making public address statements. There were a vast number of placards, 'Stop the Tour', 'Racist Swine', 'Boks Out'. There were a number of Communist banners. The only paper on sale was the *Morning Star*. It was announced that there were tickets for entry into the ground available at the organising vehicle at the front and it added 'not of course, to watch the game'. That was the comment that came over with them. One could only draw one's own conclusions about that. I didn't hear Hain's voice. I waited until the procession moved off and I followed alongside it, absorbed in the types that were in it. Their looks, their dress, what they were talking about. General appearance and so forth. And I walked all the way to Twickenham with it, where it stopped. It was very noisy. It was much more controlled than the previous demonstration on the street. It was calling out the usual slogans. It was stopped short of the ground by the police at which point I left it and went to the press box.

"In due course two groups of demonstrators emerged. I was sitting in the press box in the lower section of the main stand beside where the players came out. Away to the left is an open bank and it became clear after a while that the demonstrators had gone to that part of the ground, one group behind the goal and as far as one could estimate, there were a batch who could have been 100 to 120 strong. The other group had formed in the enclosure to the left on about the 25 yard line and they would have been about 60 or 70 in number. The group below on the left were in clear view, and I had my field glasses which are extremely powerful. I wasn't able to see everything that was happening, the group on the left were the most vociferous and the group most inclined to fight. They tried to break through the cordon of police and there were three or four inside the fence. The group on the other side were not very restive. While they were doing this, they were throwing onto the ground the odd smoke bomb or two. It was quite clear they had not worked out any strategy about where they should group because the smoke was blowing back into the stand. They were throwing flour bombs, but more dangerous they were throwing nail bombs. This was a sort of cricket ball of nails which they threw onto the ground."

Sherrard: I would have thought 'nail bombs' was getting outside the ambit of that which is pleaded.

Stable: This has been called tacks by other witnesses. We have had evidence of tacks being thrown onto the ground.

Judge: I have heard an earlier witness talk about tacks or nails.

Stable: Yes. Commander Gerrard mentioned tacks.

Sherrard: If my learned friend is saying that a bag of tacks is the same as a nail bomb then I withdraw.

Judge: This is the first time that the word bomb has been used.

Sherrard: Do you think this is the same thing?

Judge: Not the word 'bomb'.

Stable: You say the bags of tacks were about the size of cricket balls?

Wooller: They were bags which dropped onto the cricket ground at about the 25 yard line.

Stable: When a bag of tacks lands, having been thrown from the crowd onto the pitch, what does it do?

Wooller: They burst onto the ground. Fortunately the authorities had some kind of magnetic device which they used to pick these up.

Stable: As a rugby player, what did you think about this?

Wooller: In that position, it could well be that a wing of 12 or 13 stone was tackled and would incur serious injury.

Stable: Was play interrupted whilst the tacks were being removed by the magnetic device?

Wooller: Fortunately the area was cleared while play was in another area of the pitch.

Stable: Was there any stoppage?

Wooller: Very little that I recall.

Stable: Did you see any demonstrators trying to get into the ground?

Wooller: Yes, the demonstrators on my left had to be forced back. By the second half, the crowd was so incensed that there were a number of fights. The police in fact had to protect the demonstrators from the crowd.

"At Sophia Gardens, Cardiff, in January 1970, the night a number of grounds were attacked and damaged, the main Glamorgan cricket ground was broken into and a piece dug out of the square. Fortunately it could not have been done by cricketers but it was actually out of a part you play over. The score board was painted with 'Boks Out' with great daubing paint marks. The damage was done in the small hours of the morning. I was awakened early that morning by a call from the Jack de Manio programme. They had got news of the damage and I had been woken earlier by the police to tell me that there had been damage done. I was therefore up early and at about 7 o'clock I opened the front door to let my dog out and discovered that my Rover car was covered in white paint from top to bottom. It had been splashed on. It must have been done between when I went to bed at midnight and 7 o'clock."

Wooller explained who runs cricket . . .

"We had taken over at a very crucial time in the cricket world. The Cricket Council is simply a pyramid which goes through all stages of cricket down, at every level. The 17 cricket counties are well represented and I suppose the fringe membership must be a minimum of 5,000. Each county has a committee comprised of 20, 30 or 40 people so there had been a vast sounding out of public opinion throughout the cricket world and about 98%, nearly 100%, recommended that it was in the best interests of the game that England should continue to play South Africa. By this time we were under severe pressure from various anti-apartheid movements but in particular the STST movement and from what we had heard individually, it was clear that this movement intended to prevent this tour going on. After long consideration it was decided that grounds must be protected, and I think at this stage we had considered the enormous cost of this protection. It was a very difficult thing to protect a cricket ground. Also the cricket wicket is a peculiar piece of groundsmanship. It can be very easily destroyed by chemicals and it was a very difficult problem. But the cricket council decided it was their duty to go on with the tour."

And how the tour came to be cancelled . . .

"We had two meetings in that week, the first being on either the Monday or the Tuesday. Every member of the Council was present and it was decided — under pressure from various sources; outside pressures, from Government sources, indirect pressures, as you will appreciate, attempting to get the Cricket Council to cancel the tour — and we had a long and difficult discussion on this problem and we finally decided that the tour would go on, and we made a public announcement. And then the Home Secretary, James Callaghan, in conjunction with the Prime Minister, Harold Wilson at the time, intervened and we were recalled on the Thursday of that week, and we were virtually given an ultimatum to call off the tour and at the same time informed that there would be compensation paid. This turned out to be £70,000. I think it should have been £200,000 to £250,000.

"A major tour is of vital importance to the first class county. It is no secret that first class cricket has been financially unstable for a number of years. It has survived mainly because of the people who love it and work for it. One major slice of the income comes from the cricket tours. The Australians are the biggest money spinners. The Wilf Isaacs team have also become big money spinners. The South Africans were also big and we felt probably likely to be the biggest one up to that date because they have the finest cricket team in the world. The personalities were there. The cricket public wanted to see them. We had hoped it would be a very fine cricket tour and it would have raised, we had hoped, for Glamorgan, about £9,000. The county ground would have raised about £18,000. It increased our loss that season considerably."

Stable: Did Hain ever in your hearing disclaim the credit for the organisation of stopping the 1970 tour?
Wooller: No.
Stable: What did he do in relation to taking the credit for the organisation?
Wooller: The impression I got was that he was entirely the STST. It was Peter Hain.
Stable: Did he ever on the occasions when you met him expand or expound on the means he would use to do so?
Wooller: Yes, he did. He made it clear that he intended to stop the tour and at subsequent points, by any possible means.
Sherrard: You have forgotten to tell us something you told us on oath in the magistrate's court. That on the radio programme *The World at One,* that the question of damage to your car was referred to and that Mr. Hain did say that he was very sorry that it had happened and you believed him.
Wooller: Yes.
Sherrard: When Sophia Gardens at Cardiff were entered about 19 January of 1970, two students were arrested, were they not, and dealt with in magistrates' court and their names were known and published.
Wooller: Yes.
Sherrard: Mr. Wooller, the position is that you grossly exaggerated the situation that was prevailing at the time of these demonstrations into what you thought was a communist plot. Is that right? Did you say so?
Wooller: No, I said there were a lot of communists involved.
Sherrard: Did you ever read any articles about your attitude, particularly in the *Sunday Times,* about your correspondence in what was called the 'Big Red Plot Mystery'?
Wooller: Yes, I did.
Sherrard: Do you remember somebody called Michael Parkinson?
Wooller: He was a difficult person to forget.
Sherrard: Did he write articles about you in the *Sunday Times*?
Wooller: Yes.
Sherrard: Is it right that on one occasion you wrote to him in connection with the cricket tour saying, 'Dear Parkinson, I would be glad if you would inform me

whether you are a Communist or have leanings in the direction . . . "?

Wooller: Yes, I did.

Sherrard: Have you the date of that?

Wooller: February 1969.

Sherrard: Did you say to a Mr. Alex Bannister of the *Daily Mail,* in its issue of 22 October 1969 in relation to this matter — I just want to know whether this is right — is it right, Mr. Wooller, that in an interview with Mr. Alex Bannister you said, "Lefties, wierdies and odd bods . . . " . . .

Wooller: No, those are not my words. It is well known that some papers take liberties with comments.

Sherrard: Does that represent your view?

Stable: My learned friend must not say that. What the witness said was 'those were not my words'. He cannot ask whether or not he is of that opinion.

Sherrard: Sorry if I have done you an injustice. Did . . .

Judge: You cannot proceed until I have a copy of the paper you are referring to.

Sherrard: Did you say anything at all to the effect of what is set out in quotation marks "Lefties . . . " and so on?

Wooller: On 22 September the movement against the rugby tour was in its infancy and it was a just view being expressed, and I expressed the view that left-wing elements were very seriously concerned in this manoeuvre, and of course I was later to find that Mr. Hain was an extremely left-wing individual himself.

Sherrard: Do you really mean that?

Wooller: That Mr. Hain is a very left-wing liberal by his own actions and ad-missions.

Sherrard: Just let me read you something from the deposition you provided, on your oath of course, at the magistrates' court. You will find it about the second or third page of the cross-examination. I'm afraid we were not supplied with the same bundle.

Judge: When cases come before the magistrate depositions are signed at the end of the proceedings to one of which the learned counsel is now referring.

Sherrard: After reference to the Oxford Union, saying "I can produce that letter", then "I agree that on the occasion present". Do you remember that?

Wooller: Yes.

Sherrard: "I thought they made strange beafellows . . . very red".

Wooller: That is perfectly true, but I referred to Mr. Hain as a left-wing Liberal not as a Communist.

Sherrard: Would you take Mr. Hain's book and look at page 153. I am going to suggest that your whole attitude is coloured 'red' and that the jury should not attach too much weight to your view. I ask you to look at the bottom of the page. 'Our "arch-enemy" became Wilf Wooller, Secretary of the Glamorgan Cricket Club. It was largely as a result of the failure of the rugby authorities to present an articulate public representative that Mr. Wooller became spokesman for the pro-tour lobby. And his extravagant denunciations of the campaign and general aggressive manner did much to win us the support of many of the uncommitted.' Do you think you were extravagant in your denunciations of the campaign?

Wooller: No, I don't.

Sherrard: You see, Mr. Wooller, you have said in the course of your evidence given on the previous occasion that you are yourself against apartheid in sport, and I imagine therefore that you can understand that people may have very strong views about it?

Wooller: Yes, that is just.

Sherrard: Let's clear up a few matters. You didn't see Mr. Hain at Swansea, did you?

Wooller: No.

Sherrard: You didn't speak to Mr. Hain before the date we have mentioned, never on the telephone or any other way?

Wooller: My impression was that we had encountered one another on the air.

Sherrard: But not before February 1970?

Wooller: That I couldn't say.

Sherrard: Do you remember in relation to the Swansea matter, saying that about four minutes after half time, as if they had some preconceived signal, a number of demonstrators broke from the Mumbles Road end and rushed past the police and stewards? I wonder whether you will tell us whether there was a signal or not?

Wooller: I don't know. I didn't see or hear a signal, but the movement was spontaneous from an area which would have covered 50 yards of the sideline. One felt it was arranged. I could not state that there was a signal.

Sherrard: At the Oxford game, did you see Mr. Hain?

Wooller: I saw someone that I was led to understand was Mr. Hain.

Judge: The Oxford game at Twickenham?

Wooller: Yes, he came onto the pitch at Twickenham. I was given to understand that that was Mr. Hain.

Sherrard: When you got to Twickenham, that's the Barbarians game, you have told us that you heard something said over the public address system to the effect that tickets were available but not to be used for watching the game?

Wooller: That's correct, Mr. Hain was standing by the van for quite a considerable time, but to my knowledge he didn't make any announcement.

Sherrard: That announcement was made in the hearing of police officers who were supervising the demonstration?

Wooller: Yes, I would think a great number of people heard it.

Sherrard: You have told us that there was a spontaneous pelting of demonstrators by cushions. Did that happen after some preconceived signal?

Wooller: The final whistle.

Sherrard: Because you see there was a very strong counter-demonstration group against the anti-apartheid demonstrators in the ground, was there not? Another group that was against them?

Wooller: I didn't see any counter-demonstration group Just the public watching matches.

Sherrard: You never heard counter shouts. From people who were opposed to the anti-apartheid demonstrators?

Wooller: Yes, frequently, telling them to shut up.

Sherrard: Did you hear some shouts from the crowd which were meant to be offensive to coloured people?

Wooller: No, my impression was that this may well have come because I thought the demonstrators were stirring up racialism in this country, but I think the crowd were superbly well behaved, like the police.

Sherrard: Tell me this. You have given us a good many figures and details. You, as a person very much interested in these matters must have taken an interest in what the Minister of Sport was saying, at about the crucial times with which we are concerned, in the House of Commons?

Wooller: Mr. Dennis Howell.

Sherrard: Yes. Is it right that during the period with which we are concerned, it became apparent that the future of the Commonwealth Games was in danger?

Wooller: There were all sorts of rumours and statements. I cannot vouch for anything but the sports I was involved with.

Sherrard: Is it to your knowledge right that 12 out of the 18 countries who take part in the Commonwealth Games had already indicated their intention to withdraw if the cricket tour was not cancelled?

Wooller: I cannot vouch for this.

Sherrard: Let me read from the Minister's speech on this issue.

Stable: May I know to what end this is?

Sherrard: If the figures that my learned friend has introduced with regard to revenue are relevant then in my submission the figures of revenue on the other side are clearly relevant. All I understand my learned friend was doing was pointing out how much was lost due to the cancellation. I wish to point out how much would have been lost had the tour not been cancelled.

Judge: I don't think they are the same thing at all. The figures Mr. Stable referred to are relevant to this indictment. I don't see that yours are in any way relevant to this matter.

Sherrard: Were you aware that over £4m would be lost in the event that the Commonwealth Games hadn't taken place?

Stable: To what issue before the jury and in what way does it show whether Mr. Hain was party to agreements using lawful or unlawful means to achieve this end? These are the points before the jury and I don't see the relevance.

Sherrard: Because it is quite wrong for a case to be presented with a financial picture representing one aspect of the campaign against the cricket tour if they are prevented from considering the material on the other side. If you have one aspect, it is clear in my submission that one must consider the other side.

Judge: I understand the relevance to figures and costs referred to in relation to unlawful conduct on the part of the demonstrators. These are relevant. But this series of questions on which you are now embarking seem to be in a different category. I entertain very much doubt as to whether this is relevant, but I am not going to stop you putting it if you feel it is of importance.

Sherrard: Would you tell me, Mr. Wooller, whether or not you were aware of the representations which were made to the Cricket Council in relation to the threat to the Commonwealth Games in Edinburgh?

Wooller: We were not concerned with that. Our sport is multi-racial. We could not concern ourselves with the activities of another sport.

Sherrard: I didn't ask whether you concerned yourself. Were there any represen-
tations to you about it?
Wooller: I don't recall. At that time there was a great deal of feeling being whipped
up in a number of the African countries.
Sherrard: Do you remember a representative coming from Edinburgh to a meeting?
A Mr. Alex Ross?
Wooller: We had somebody but I can't remember his name.
Sherrard: Did he come to a meeting at Lords?
Wooller: He could have done.
Sherrard: Did he say how endangered were the Commonwealth Games and how
serious the matter would be if they were cancelled?
Wooller: He might well have done. I can't recall a Mr. Ross but it would have been
part of the evidence.
Sherrard: You said that 98% majority were in favour of the continuation of the
tour in the cricket world. But that's not right, is it?
Wooller: I emphasise in the cricket world, and that's all we were judging on.
Sherrard: You are not suggesting are you, Mr. Wooller, that people had forgotten
the D'Oliveira affair which had blown up earlier?
Wooller: I hope not.
Sherrard: There was a very large meeting of the MCC, was there not, and even if we
take the MCC line the resolutions then with regard to the South African tour and
the protests with regard to Mr. D'Oliveira were certainly not defeated by anything
like 98%, were they?
Wooller: There are two matters. The stopping or the furtherance of the tour is one
matter, and what happened to Mr. D'Oliveira is another.
Sherrard: I am suggesting that it was the same issue because as time went on more
people in the cricket world were coming round to the view that was being expressed.
Wooller: I would say the contrary. They were turning more and more to back the
cricket world.
Sherrard: I must put it to you that in fact what was happening was that the mem-
bership were becoming more concerned with the humanitarian side?
Wooller: We have no evidence to support that.

Discussing a debate at the Oxford Union which he had with Hain, Wooller said
that Hain spoke very strongly about using all means possible to achieve the end of
stopping the cricket tour.

Sherrard: Do you remember it being made absolutely plain that the object of the
exercise was that the game would stop, not that people would fall in the tacks?
Wooller: The object of Hain's thing was to stop all games.
Judge: If someone throws tacks onto the pitch in this way, unless he gives prior
notice they would be treading on those things before they were aware of their
presence.
Sherrard: What I am suggesting is that they were thrown with a view to stopping
the game. What I am saying is that they were thrown not to hurt players but to
force the game to be stopped.
Judge: In the form of a question, asking Mr. Wooller about that, that would be

for the jury to decide. They will be able to listen to the evidence and decide to what end the tacks were thrown onto the pitch.

Sherrard: Do you suggest that Mr. Hain ever uttered a word of encouragement to anyone to throw tacks in your presence?

Wooller: To throw tacks no, but to stop the game, yes.

Sherrard: Short of violence?

Wooller: He always said he was against violence but he referred to petrol bombs in the Robin Day programme.

Sherrard: Are you suggesting that Mr. Hain advocated throwing petrol bombs?

Wooller: No.

Sherrard: Mr. Wooller, I suggest . . .

Stable: What he is saying is that Mr. Hain made it perfectly clear on occasions in Mr. Wooller's hearing that he would stop at nothing to stop the tour or whatever it was he was trying to stop at that time. He then went on to say that he was against violence and during the Robin Day *Panorama* programme he referred to petrol bomb throwing and said he was against that. That's a summary of what he said and my learned friend immediately picked him up on the basis that he had talked about throwing petrol bombs on the programme.

Sherrard: We all apologise if we did you an injustice. There is no question is there that Mr. Hain was in any way approving violence, tacks, petrol bombs or any other bombs?

Judge: Approving is ambiguous.

Sherrard: Did you hear Mr. Hain —

Wooller: I didn't hear Mr. Hain advocate violence.

Sherrard's extraction from Wooller that, although he had debated with Hain about the tactics used to try and stop the rugby and cricket tour, the young man had never advocated violence, was a blow to the prosecution's case — that direct action tactics, although couched in the language of non-violence, inevitably led to violence and anarchy. So Stable was quickly on his feet in re-examination of the witness in an attempt to recover the lost ground.

Stable: You have said that in your hearing Mr. Hain, without specifically mentioning the use of tacks, had said that he would use any means to stop the tour?

Wooller: Yes, that he made absolutely clear on many occasions.

Stable: You have also said that you have never heard him advocate violence?

Wooller: That is true.

Stable: So that we can be quite clear as to what your meaning is, do you regard both those answers as consistent with each other?

Wooller: No.

Stable: Could you just explain in your own words how you have heard Mr. Hain answer the question of the means he was to use, or was prepared to use, to stop the tour?

Wooller: Invading the pitch, sitting down, flashing mirrors and all sorts of things like that. At one point somebody in the North was going to come down with a batch of locusts. He always made it clear that he would stop the tour and it was clear that there would be a very sharp clash between opposing factions which would lead to trouble.

Sherrard: I am sorry to intervene, but is Mr. Wooller saying that Mr. Hain was advocating the use of mirrors and the use of locusts?

Wooller: No, they were merely mentioned in the activities of the STST.

Stable: By him or in his presence?

Wooller: I would say in his presence. I can't recall any words he used, but his implication was clear, that he would stop the tour.

Judge: You did say a few moments ago that this involved sitting down, flashing mirrors, etc. When you gave that evidence were you referring to words you heard spoken by Mr. Hain?

Wooller: Yes, they were spoken by him and in the same place that we were in together.

Stable: Would it be fair to summarise what you have said about this that really you have heard him advocate any means short of actual violence?

Wooller: That would summarise my views.

CHAPTER IX

"I did not seek this Platform"

So far the evidence had been entirely predictable. Virtually nothing which had not been reported during the demonstrations of 1969 and 1970 had emerged. Significantly missing was conspiratorial evidence. Had this been a Crown case the Special Branch would have testified to meetings held, and by whom what decisions were made, and so on, for they had kept the STST movement under close surveillance during the campaigns. Bennion, with none of this information, had to rely on turns of phrase in Hain's book such as "We were organising long into the night" (p. 130); "at one stage I had 400 tickets hidden in my bedroom" (p. 141); and "as we had planned, the Commonwealth Games issue was blowing up". (p. 179)

Bennion was expected in the witness box to hammer home his conspiracy allegations. But on August 3 Stable let it be known that he was not going to call Bennion, who had given evidence in the magistrates' court at the committal proceedings.

"There is no issue before the jury on which he can give relevant evidence", said Stable. "He was called primarily to produce evidence of authorship of the book. He was also called to give evidence which went to a count to which the magistrates didn't commit Hain. And there is nothing else on which he can give relevant evidence. I have him here should the defence wish to call him, but I am not proposing to call him nor to tender him in cross-examination."

Sherrard, exploding with rage, barked: "Is he suggesting that because he won't call the prosecutor that I should?"

Stable: No.

Sherrard: This is staggering. I will consider it overnight.

Stable: I am perfectly well aware what my duty is to the court. It is limited to having the prosecutor available to give evidence if the defence wishes.

Francis Bennion sat with arms folded two rows behind the prosecutor "scarcely seeming even to blink, as if he were carved from polished wood", as Corinna Adam described his demeanour in the *New Statesman.*

That evening Hain decided to defend himself. It was a decision taken after consultation with his lawyers, his family and closest friends. Bennion's non-appearance had little or nothing to do with it; the deciding factor was the judge's decision to allow count four of the charges — which when the pleas were taken at the outset of the trial he had rejected as unsound — to be re-introduced. This count accused Hain of conspiring to prevent and cause to be cancelled the 1970 cricket tour by unlawful means. (For full wording see appendices.) Hain saw the Judge's decision to allow the fourth count *after* hearing all the prosecution evidence, coupled with Sherrard's trenchant and well-argued opposition to this, as indicating that the Judge was entirely against his side. It seemed the only alternative was to attempt to go over the Judge's head to the jury and perhaps secure a perverse verdict if not an outright acquittal. The legal jungle which the Judge and four lawyers were creating was becoming so dense that the jury could not hope to see through it, and so, he reasoned, a commonsense or instinctive verdict was possible. Sherrard and Capstick opposed Hain's dismissal of them, as officially — given Bar Council ethics — they were bound to. But a growing despair and cynicism in Sherrard's court attitude made it seem likely that he was not too sorry to be out of the case.

Bennion's side took the news of the changed defence tactics without any visible or vocal sign. Privately they were flabbergasted, as their preparation for the case had been on the certainty that Hain would have to give sworn evidence. Also it becomes a Judge's duty to 'protect' a person defending himself and — provided the switch was made diplomatically — the jury might sympathise with the underdog, particularly one of this defendant's youth and burning sincerity which the prosecution had repeatedly promised not to challenge.

So on that Friday morning, with the trial two weeks old, Hain took charge of his own destiny. Bowing out, Sherrard told the Judge that Hain wished to defend himself because he was more familiar with the realities of the case than anyone else, and "we understand and respect his point of view". Judge Gillis was clearly perturbed by this turn of events and strove to persuade Hain to change his mind. "Whether a defendant is represented by counsel or not is always a matter for his final, exclusive decision and nothing I am about to say is in any way qualifying that undoubted right," he said, whereupon he launched into a lengthy homily.

He praised the manner in which the defence had so far presented its case. Matters of law and facts had arisen and the advice and experience of counsel were necessary. Grant (Hain's solicitor) could remain in court but he had no 'right of audience'. The extent to which Hain's decision had shaken Judge Gillis was indicated when he remarked that he did not know "whether he is a graduate of law or had any legal qualification in any country". Hain would receive every assistance the court could properly give him but the same rules of evidence and procedure would apply.

"I recognise the sincerity behind his anxiety to say what he thinks is right, but he must remember that this is not a public meeting. The uprightness of the cause does not in my view allow any person to set aside the rule of law", said Judge Gillis who then adjourned the court for 20 minutes for Hain to reconsider.

Hain had coffee with his advisers but barely discussed the issue during the interval. His mind was made up the previous evening: it was anyway an action he had been cogitating for months. Sherrard told the judge that his client wished to continue in person. "We shall go and watch from the pavillion", he said as he and Capstick walked out. Capstick said "Cheerio" to Hain and left a pile of papers and law books for the young defendant. It was an eerie moment. On the right hand side of the imposing Lord Chief Justice's Court sat Hain alone in the two rows of pews reserved for barristers. In the solicitor's row in the well of the court sat Larry Grant, his solicitor, and Geoff Robertson, an adviser on the defence, with Yvette Gibson, Grant's secretary, taking notes and fishing out documents.

On the prosecution side sat Owen Stable, QC, Brian Potter, his junior counsel, Francis Bennion (who is a non-practising barrister) and his solicitor and two clerks. It was not surprising that in his opening words Hain's voice faltered a little and was inaudible. But once he had assessed the necessary pitch of voice needed in the lofty court he sailed away. An experienced speaker from the public platform and a seminar debater, Hain used the latter technique for the trial as he fought to avoid a likely prison sentence.

Judge Gillis was still bothered by the young man in brown sports jacket and corduroy trousers standing in the barrister's bench in the Lord Chief Justice's Court. "Strictly a litigant in person should stand in the well of the court but I will let you sit there," he conceded. Had he in fact put Hain in the well of the giant court it would, of course, have been almost impossible for him to conduct a defence.

All that remained of the prosecution's case was to read the evidence from the magistrates' court of S.C. Griffiths, the secretary of the MCC and of the Test and County Cricket Board and of the Cricket Council. He said the International Cricket Conference (to which South Africa had not belonged since it left the Commonwealth) at its meeting in 1966 had confirmed the invitation to South Africa to tour England in 1970. He described much the same events and views within the Cricket Council as Wilfrid Wooller had done. The important part of his evidence concerned a letter from Hain to himself. It read:

"Dear Mr. Griffith,

The issue of racialism in sport is one which is becoming increasingly important throughout the world, and in Britain has received considerable public attention over the past two months.

"It is against this background that we believe the MCC Council should view the coming tour by a white South African cricket team. The fact that this team is representative of only a small minority of South Africans is well known, as is the denial of opportunities and facilities to non-white cricketers.

"By continuing to play host to a team chosen on a racialist basis, the MCC is condoning racialism and the importation of apartheid politics into cricket.

"The protests against the present Rugby team have indicated the strength of feeling against racialist sport amongst a significant section of the population – from demonstrators at Twickenham, to miners in Wales and clergymen in Manchester.

"The consequences of another refusal to cancel the 1970 tour cannot be over emphasised. The strength of our campaign has been demonstrated on the Rugby tour. Cricket is far more susceptible to non-violent direct action than rugby. Should the tour take place, next year's cricket season could degenerate into chaos with protests and disruptions at every match.

"Local branches of the 'STST' have sprung up throughout the country in action against the rugby tour and in preparation for the cricket tour. Even if the MCC is not prepared itself to take a moral stand against racialism in cricket and call off the tour, the MCC Council ought seriously to consider the practical conseqeuences of staging it."

A good omen for the defence, virtually its first, came almost immediately afterwards. Judge Gillis said he was not satisfied that there was evidence connecting Hain to the particular in count one connecting with "driving away of coaches". Stable replied that the book had given a description of the incident outside the Park

Lane Hotel and referred to the words "at planning meetings before" the incident. The Judge replied: "As you know, when persons in a conspiracy are alleged to be party to wrong acts, there has to be evidence linking them in the matter of criminal responsibility to the accused of every act complained of . . . It is so exiguous and narrow I would prefer to delete it." Stable's offer to take the words out was accepted.

Hain rose to his feet and spent the next hour outlining his defence. The Judge punctuated it with well-meaning interruptions which Hain appeared to use to get his breath and glance at his notes, yet was never too preoccupied to forget to thank the Judge for his guidance. He told the jury:

"In opening the defence I would like to make one thing perfectly clear and that is that prior to Bennion's laying these summonses I have never been in a court, let alone being in the position of defending myself in one of the highest courts in the land, and I hope you will bear with me if I go wrong. I should point out that I am not in this court by choice and that relates to the view expressed by the Judge earlier on in connection with the court not being a public meeting. I did not seek this platform. I also want to make clear that I don't want to be a martyr and so I feel I must defend myself and convince you and the court that I am not guilty of the offences alleged.

"I accept the book as evidence, and I stand broadly by what I wrote in it. I don't withdraw that. I believe that it does paint a broadly accurate picture of the campaign and of the whole issue of apartheid in sport. I believe it also paints a broadly accurate picture of the events, in which I played a small part only, which lead to the cancellation of the 1970 tour. I feel that I should point out that the book was written about six to eight months after the events it chronicled, so that I have found out that some of the things described are not strictly accurate. But I believe they are minor ones — the inaccuracies — and do not effect the broad over-all picture.

"I would also like to point out at this stage that, having said I accept the book, it is not a confession. I did not write it with Sherrard or Stable or any other lawyer standing by my side watching every sentence I wrote. This is perhaps a very important point. I had no idea whatsoever when I wrote the book that it would be used two years later in evidence against me. And I would have considered a little more carefully the way I described certain incidents and my alleged role in those incidents if I had known that it was going to be dissected, not merely sentence by sentence but word by word. I did not have a lawyer to vet each sentence. I would also like to make clear that the book was written for readability, not as a legal submission. I am not disputing that it is evidence in this case. I am saying that it was not written with the intention of being evidence in this case. I hope you will bear that in mind.

"Because the consideration is not so much what is actually said in the book, but what interpretation you put on it. And I would put a very different interpretation on the sentences which have been read out to you — on the book as a whole — than, naturally, that which Stable has put. There have been a number of very selective extracts from the book so far. I would seek in defending myself, in calling the witnesses I intend to call, to show to you that there is another side to the picture which has been painted. That there is not merely another side, but that there are extracts in the book which clearly show there is another side.

"I also feel it necessary to say at this stage, although I think this point has probably come out and been registered, that I am completely opposed to violence.

70

I am opposed to violence because I have lived in South Africa and I have experienced, and so has my family, the violence of apartheid. And that has led me quite deliberately to the view that violence is wrong and I am committed to non-violence. Violence, when you see it, is a very nasty thing, and in my view we have talked very glibly about that.

"In my role as public spokesman for the campaign — a role, you will remember, which was described as having arisen from being 'elected by the press' — in this role I have consistently advocated non-violence. When I spoke at a public meeting there were always those who got up and said, 'Why don't you advocate violence?' and I remember constantly having this disagreement in open public meetings, because I do speak in this role throughout the country. Even the prosecution witnesses agree on this point. Wooller and Winter stressed this. The same views on violence apply to my views on malicious damage. I will be submitting in my defence that there is no evidence whatsoever to connect me with any malicious damage, that I consistently continued this throughout the campaign, and that with particular examples as they arose I had no connection, and I will bring witnesses I hope to convince you of that."

Judge Gillis here interrupted Hain to say: "When we use the word malicious damage we mean damage intentionally and deliberately done, not spitefully done. You say you were never party to doing any deliberate or intentional damage?"

Hain replied: "I do and I make that point as strongly as I do the one about non-violence. I think it is morally wrong, and I stress morally wrong, to dig up cricket grounds, but that it is also politically counter-productive to the anti-apartheid cause. I also wish to stress that I am not a law-breaker and I wish to repudiate very definitely the image that has been foisted on me during this prosecution, which you may have read about and which others certainly have read about, and which you have heard from Stable. I have never equated my beliefs with law-breaking and I hope that you will judge this case and my position in that light.

"I find the prosecution's allegations on this point — because you will remember that what they sought to do was to equate the terms 'non-violent direct action' with law-breaking — and I find the way and the manner in which that was expressed was that I was put in a position where I was advocating the laws of the jungle. No one has ever accused me of that before. I find that insulting. By the end of the case I hope I will have been able to convince you that my views are the true and accurate ones. I am not disputing that events took place which may have been of an unconventional nature — and I use that word in preference to Stable's 'unlawful' — and I wish to stress that these were not on my part unlawful. I did not seek to stop the tour — which you will remember was a lawful objective — I did not seek to do that by illegal means. And I don't think the prosecution has shown that I did.

"I will be submitting, too, that the campaign was a loose movement. It was not a rigid organisation. We had no generals. We had no apparatus through which to conspire. It was a loose movement of individuals who felt that the issues raised by these racialist sports were an affront to them and were of such significance that they were obliged to register their moral protest in the way they felt best able to do. And I will be calling a number of witnesses to say that they acted completely spontaneously of their own accord — that they had never even met me, let alone conspired with me.

"I will also be calling your attention to the book, page 196. This, you remember, is a page which has not been read to you before:

'The movement itself was very loose and based entirely on local initiative and commitment. At its base were the local action groups – in all, about 400 by the time of the cancellation. These groups were autonomous in both organisation and policy. Then there were the regional centres which, during the cricket campaign, assumed complete responsibility for organising protests at each tour centre. Finally, there was the National Committee which, in many ways, holds the key to an understanding of the nature of STST.'

There was also a point which arose from the judge's statement to Stable that there must be evidence linking the accused with every one of the events complained of and I submit that there is not that evidence because of the spontaneity of that campaign, and because local people – individuals – acted under their own inspiration."

Judge: You should understand that part of the function of the jury in considering matters of fact is to draw such *inferences* that they feel convinced from the facts brought before them. The law doesn't consider, in dealing with conspiracy, that there should be evidence of a witness to say, I heard the accused agree with another accused to do what is complained of. The only evidence usually in conspiracy is evidence of facts that if proved the prosecution invites the jury to infer evidence of conspiracy. The law doesn't require that there should be express evidence that you were seen doing any of these acts, if there is evidence that would justify the jury in concluding that you were party to them.

Hain: That I agreed to them. Yes, I understand that. I don't need to go into the issues surrounding this campaign at this stage, because you have probably read them in the book, and have heard some of the passages read out which express the general principles. I think you will agree that this was an honest campaign and that as spokesman I always made my views quite clear on the issues that were involved. They were published – and in a sense that is why I alone am standing before you. Because perhaps the reason behind the prosecution is that I am the only person known to be identified with the campaign. But I make the point that it was an honest campaign.

Also, I was never charged with any offence. I realise this isn't the whole issue – and that whether I was charged at the time may not enter into the issue, but I think it is worth recording that when I made these statements throughout the campaign there was no suggestion that I would be prosecuted on a summary charge or a conspiracy charge. Indeed you might have heard that I have had very friendly relations with the police. In my submission to accept the prosecution case would be to pretend that I was some kind of political superstar. To pretend that I was capable on the indictment of agreeing to what Sherrard described, in the first count alone, as 147 different particulars. That is a considerable achievement. I don't think I was capable of it even if I had wanted to do it. My role was as a public spokesman and that alone. There are many other people who responded to that campaign.

Judge: One matter you may be under misapprehension about. At the end of the prosecution case it is the duty of the judge to see that no allegation goes before the jury unless there is in his opinion in matter of law matters fit for their consideration. That led me to strike out references to driving away coaches. When the jury give their verdict, if it comes to that, there is no necessity that they have to be convinced of each and every particular of alleged unlawful conduct. It is sufficient if they are satisfied that the prosecution have convinced them as to your guilt in respect of any of the four charges. I thought you might think that all particulars had to be proved.

Hain: The prosecution, in bringing this case, relied very heavily on the term 'nation-wide conspiracy'. This was something that Stable repeated again and again and it is my submission that not only was there no nationwide conspiracy but that such a thing, in the context of these offences, would have been impossible, because of the structure of the movement or because of the lack of structure, that it was very loose, that it did lack a rigid chain of command, that it lacked any chain of command. We had lengthy arguments of legal technicalities of the indictment, and in those argu-ments Stable relied very heavily again on the terms 'a nationwide conspiracy' so that you could get everything under that, because the objective of stopping the tour is not illegal.

I am disputing that there was a nationwide conspiracy. And not only that, but that I was no party to any conspiracy whatsoever. I will be calling many witnesses to show that this argument is one which is valid and one that I ask this court to accept. I could call 50,000 witnesses if I wanted to – that is the number given in the book as having acted in support of opposition to this tour. What I do intend to do is to call individuals to give evidence to this court who have acted of their own accord. Who had not even met me when they took a particular action. I think it is right at this stage to direct your attention to the full magnitude of the offences alleged against me.

The judge has pointed out the particular aspect which I now accept and under-stand. So that if I am found guilty of any one of the particulars I am guilty of the whole lot. And I must seek to convince you that not only was there no nationwide conspiracy, but that in addition many individuals acted complete independently of me and any 'nationwide conspiracy'. There was massive opposition ranging from trade unionists to housewives to students to political activists. I am not saying it was a majority, it was a minority, but you should bear in mind the extent of the opposition so that you may judge, in view of the mass of allegations against me, so that you may judge in the context of many, many people taking action quite spontaneously both as individuals and through their own organisations – that you can judge in that context of massive opposition to the tour whether you will find me guilty or not. I must say in terms of the context, because I think that is ter-ribly important.

Naturally we have got to get down to the nitty-gritty of seeing whether I com-mitted any offences alleged, but the context is important so that you can have a coherent view of what I am alleged to have done. I think also it is relevant to make the distinction between being in agreement with a particular act that an in-dividual may have done – and I do not retract from my views, and they are set out in the book, as to what I though was the proper course – I want to make the distinction between my identifying with an act (for example, the witness I

73

will call who ran onto the pitch completely on his own), between my identifying with him and agreeing with him to do that. I may agree in the sense that I identify with something that somebody has done independently, but that is not to say that I agreed with him to do it; conspired with him. That distinction is very important. Conspiracy is a very, very wide law. It simply means that you are in agreement to do an act.

My final point is this: I have been accused of arrogance and intolerance. I don't say this with any arrogance or intolerance. My conscience in this campaign is clear. I don't retract my role in it. I believe I acted in the correct manner in my role as spokesman. My conscience is clear because we were asserting a principle of fundamental human justice — non-racialism. And secondly my conscience is clear because I am not guilty.

Judge Gillis was plainly disconcerted about Hain's decision not to go into the witness box himself and give sworn evidence. It may be that he thought Hain had found a way of circumventing the snags of going into the witness box by conducting his own defence. Hain told the Judge that his main reason for not giving evidence was that he had nothing to add to the book which was "the core of the evidence".

Judge Gillis pounced: "You misunderstand. There is no evidence before the jury other than matters already in evidence. If you do not give sworn evidence then all that is in evidence before the jury is that which has come from the lips of witnesses or what is contained in documents and pictures. It may be that the course you want to follow is to go into the witness box and say that what you have told the jury in your opening speech is the truth and offer yourself for cross examination. I want you to understand that so far you have given no evidence.."

Hain would not budge, arguing: "The case for the prosecution rests essentially on my book. I admit to having written the book, and I admit to what is in it. I don't really have anything personally to add. What I wish to do is to explain through witnesses I call what the book means. You will recall that when this prosecution was sought to be brought the book was relied upon. Shortly after the book having been published Bennion laid his summonses. That clearly is a matter on which he rests. I rest on it too."

Judge: In the book there are a number of matters to which the prosecution have invited the attention of the jury, and they have submitted that what is meant by the passages they have read was the matters they put before the jury. For example, one of the submissions of Stable was that in the context of the book what you were meaning by direct action is in effect non-violent *unlawful* action. You can of course argue on the book in a different way. But if you want to give evidence as to what you were meaning by it that has to be by spoken evidence.

This legal pedantry did not shake Hain even though the Judge kept up his attempt to persuade him he was mistaken.

"The example I gave", said Judge Gillis, "is only one of many submissions on the book that I gather you are not accepting. I want you to appreciate that if you want to make what is your understanding of what you meant when you wrote the book clear that has to come by way of evidence. You cannot say to the jury, I meant this when I said that. That is a statement of fact, and   statements of fact have to be made in the witness box."

Hain's reply was: "It seems to me that the book is obvious in its interpretation and that it ought to be taken at face value." Judge Gillis tried three more lines of argument but gave up in the face of Hain's refusal to be swayed by legalisms and the authority of the judge. "I appreciate that the prosecution case is founded on the book and that all other witnesses called are ancillary to that", said Hain finally.

Lawyers said later that Judge Gillis came close to using improper pressure on Hain by his constant attempts to persuade him not to defend himself and his attempts to alter Hain's decision not to go into the witness box.

CHAPTER X

Matters of Conscience

It was with some relief when, after all the legal battles, surprises and tensions of the previous two days, a common-or-garden witness at last reached the stand. Yet if William Laithwaite had an ordinary appearance and occupation he certainly was no commonplace character. He told the jury that he was aged 65 and a life-long sportsman, having played rugby, cricket, swimming, cycling, in fact "done pretty well everything". He had played rugby until he was 58 in the junior team at Sutton.

"When the South Africa rugby team arrived in 1969 I felt that condoning the tour of a team which was chosen not on the basis of one's ability or sportsmanship but on the basis of the colour of one's skin was alien to the very precepts of good sportsmanship. The form of social organisation in South Africa was alien to the basic ideas of democratic control which I hold. I believe that it (the regime) is philosophically and ethically immoral, and whilst it may economically have short-term advantages it will be disastrous. I have watched every important game at Twickenham since 1944 and I felt a considerable affront at finding the Oxford game switched to Twickenham.

"When I felt my home in Sutton that mroning I couldn't see what I could possibly do. I knew there would be a good deal of police in attendance, but as one little man I had no idea what to do. But I picked up my own rugby bag with the kit in it and took it to the office. But as time went on I still couldn't think of any tactics. But then I noticed a bottle of red ink and realised I had on a white shirt. I took my shirt off, put a red AA on it, put my pullover back on and went to the ground, kidding the man at the door that I was a linesman. By that means I managed to get onto the field and show that I objected. I didn't wish to break any law and didn't wish to cause any violence, and so, although I was very seriously provoked in the middle of the field by the referee, who cast some doubt on my parentage, I left.

"Just before I did so I was approached by Laidlaw, a very magnificent New Zealand player, who pointed out that he had only come here to play rugby and I said I have come here to protest because there were very many more important things here than rugby. We then agreed to talk later; that was not possible however. But we did exchange letters and I was delighted to learn from the press now that Laidlaw refuses to play rugby on the New Zealand team against a visiting South African team."

Laithwaite told the court that when officials turned up with policemen he didn't want to break any law or engage in any punch-up so he left the pitch with them. He was not charged with any offence. The real reason he had run on the pitch, he added, was to honour Braam Fischer, a South African lawyer now serving life imprisonment in Pretoria central prison for conspiracy against the state. He had read his "really magnificent" statement at the trial and "I came on that field out of respect for Fischer."

He added that he had felt somewhat uncertain whether he was doing the right thing until he got into the middle of the pitch. He made a second attempt at the international match on 20 December. "With the aid of two plates of oranges and lemons I got through the main door and I was ready to go onto the field when I am afraid I was recognised by the men on the field." He had never discussed either protest with Hain, nor anybody. "I didn't know myself I was going to do it."

Under cross-examination by Stable, Laithwaite agreed he knew about the general wave of protests going on against the tour. Instantly we were at the real point of the trial.

Stable: Having regard to your views about apartheid, that provided the line is drawn against actual physical violence to any spectator who isn't there for the purpose of demonstrating, or any player or organiser, really anything goes?
Laithwaite: As a democratic right to protest.
Judge: Counsel isn't asking you about that. You are being asked whether your view is that any action short of actual physical violence can be done on such an occasion. Not merely protest. He is asking you about conduct. Whether you draw your line just short of actual physical violence. Put the question again.
Stable: Would I be right in saying that you draw the line at actual physical violence towards either spectators, players or organisers, but having drawn that line would I be right in thinking that your view is that really everything up to, but short of, actual physical violence is all right?
Laithwaite: Correct.

Laithwaite agreed that as a member of the Sutton branch of the Anti-Apartheid Movement he was part of a national group. He was not aware that AAM was officially connected to STST. He had found Hain's name and address on a small pamphlet and had phoned up and later sent a donation after the rugby tour started.

Stable: So that really from the very start of the rugby tour you knew that Hain was seeking to promote demonstrations, to co-ordinate activities of various groups?
Laithwaite: I can't answer that question, because I have no idea or conception of what organisations those were. Just that it was a protest movement.

The next witness for the defence never really got going because the prosecution objected that he was stating beliefs and not facts. Neil Edward Wates, who lives in Dulwich, a rich suburb which is next to two ghetto areas of Brixton and Camberwell, is the managing director of the giant building concern, Wates Ltd. He said he and others had written to the *Times* protesting about the intended cricket tour. Between the constant arguments between the Judge, Hain and Stable he managed to say: "I was in South Africa when the tour was cancelled, and I felt the dismay and the laager mentality of the people there. And, of course, I heard what was said about you, the extreme hostility to you. You were made the scapegoat." The cross-examination of Wates by Stable was revealing of the prosecution strategy and illustrated if anything did that a skilled barrister may ask the most far-reaching questions provided he casts them within the manner accepted by court tradition.

Stable: You feel strongly about the impropriety of some of the laws of South Africa, particularly in relation to their coloured population. Do you agree that besides that issue there are very serious issues upon which sincere and honest people can hold very strong views?

Wates: Yes.

Stable: Do you accept that there is a large body of opinion in this country that is appalled by the treatment by the Russian government against the Jewish members of that country? Similarly of the way Kenyan Asians, Vietnamese, intellectuals behind the Iron Curtain are treated?

Wates: I accept all this.

Stable: These are all serious matters about which honest men can feel strongly. Do you consider that in relation to those matters every single person in this country may do whatever he thinks might alleviate the problem by any means he chooses provided he keeps within the law of England?

Wates: Yes.

Stable: May I take it that however strongly you feel about apartheid the line that you yourself would draw would be the line drawn by the law?

Wates: Of course.

Stable: And would your philosophy be that everything that the law allows is in and everything outside the law is out?

Wates: Yes.

Stable: Do you agree that unless the overwhelming majority of the citizens of this country — all of whom probably feel strongly about one or the other of the things I have mentioned — unless the line which the law draws is the line which the majority of the citizens accept as being the right line that chaos would result?

Wates: Yes.

Stable: Do you agree with me that if everybody who felt deeply and burningly sincerely about a particular question and said, I feel so strongly about this that I needn't consider what the law has to say —

Hain: Objection. If I am not allowed to put a question to him about apartheid I don't see how Stable can put a question about Russian Jews.

Judge: These are preliminary questions Stable is putting to come to a question that is going to affect the evidence.

Stable: Do you agree with me that if a person who feels very strongly about a particular matter in relation to that matter was able to say to himself, this to me is so important that I can disregard the limits set by the law, that if we all did that the whole of our freedom and indeed parliamentary democracy would be at an end?

Wates: I agree.

The issue of conscience was never more clearly exemplified in this trial than in the next witness' evidence. A blunt young man called Gerrard Murray, the deputy president of Leicester University Students Union, he had at the time of the rugby tour been vice-president responsible for external affairs. He was a rugby player.

Murray told the court that at the Students Union Council on 9 October 1969 he seconded a motion which was passed instructing the Council to write to Leicester Football Club asking them to cancel the South African match on their ground. A month later a general meeting of the students passed a strongly-worded motion calling for a demonstration. The Vice-Chancellor supported the idea. Out of 3,000 students at the university, 800 came to the meeting, the largest he had seen. The university rugby club decided not to sell tickets for the game as it would have normally done. Murray said that an amendment was proposed to the main motion suggesting that the word 'peaceful' be inserted in front of the word 'demonstration'. Only 25 voted for this amendment and it was lost by an overwhelming majority.

Murray explained why the amendment was rejected. "Feeling was very, very high. It had been made worse — and this was why we rejected the word 'peaceful' — because both myself and the president had received threats from the National Front, and also they had said that they would muster their own Midlands force to see that the demonstrations did not take place. We felt that it was wrong to have the word peaceful because we felt that everyone had the right to his self-defence."

Judge: Did you understand by that resolution that you were agreeing if need be to use non-peaceful, unlawful methods?
Murray: Yes, I think everybody did.

The witness said another motion was passed offering support for demonstrations in other towns against Springbok games on the same terms. "We were saying that one expects demonstrations will normally be peaceful but that when you are faced with bodies like the National Front you can't say it will be peaceful."

Hain asked Murray whether he had any contact with him.

Murray: Not up till then. After this I rang up and spoke to Peter Hain's mother and told her of our proposed demonstration and said if he wanted to come he would be welcome. I had called all kinds of officials of students unions and invited a number of people to come. It was just one of many phone calls. The background to the motions passed by the students was completely independent of Hain. After the demonstration against the Leicester match had broken up and people were leaving, somebody pointed out that you were Peter Hain. I then went over and introduced myself. That was the first time I met him. Between 3-4,000 people demonstrated at Leicester, coming from Manchester, Swansea, Leeds as well, against a team that had been picked on racial lines. There was just a revulsion at that. Normal human revulsion.

"Not all the people on the march were political activists. I was the chief marshall and among my stewards were the president of the Aquinas Club, the catholic club, two players from the second XV, and members of the Conservative Association. There was a complete range of views represented. It was remarkably quiet and peaceful. There was a bit of a fracas when the National Front broke through the police lines and started lashing about with banners, but the police made no arrests on either side. Apart from the one incident it was quiet."

Murray took exception to Hain's description in his book that the Leicester game had taken place in "an atmosphere of siege" and quarrelled with Hain's loose terms such as "the movement had shown its strength". He asked: "What movement? The sentence does not make sense. The movement included many people. In that sense the movement had already been there. We just organised for the movement. I had no card to say I belonged to STST, AAM or anything. It was just ordinary people."

Describing his first meeting with Hain, Murray said: "I came over and introduced myself and said how frustrated and disheartened I felt about that afternoon's proceedings. You turned around to me and said it was tremendous and that it was fine. To which I thought, this was typical of the political persuasion Hain represented, and I actually said, 'typical of a bloody Liberal'. It was typical of the whole philosophy you represented."

The tension between Hain and his own witness flared further when Hain asked Murray: "Had I made the statement that appears in the book ('the movement had shown its strength') at that time, being the local organiser of the demonstration, what would your view have been?"

Murray: I would have felt, have your ego trip somewhere else. If there is any praise due it is due to the president and myself who had done the organising.

Hain: On page 131 of the book when I say, 'establishing good working contact' you appreciate that this is quite an important phrase in relation to the alleged conspiracy that I am charged with. Could you describe what that meant?

Murray: That meant we got from time to time letters through the post asking for money, then pamphlets, then another letter asking for money. It meant nothing more than that. It did not involve passing down of instructions to us. We sent coaches of students to demonstrations at Manchester and Swansea and I don't think we notified you. We acted completely spontaneously.

Stable rose for his cross-examination of this witness with a glint in his eye. Here was a straight-talking young man well to the left of Hain politically and there had been some needle between them.

Stable: You were an undergraduate at Leicester in 1969. Are you now a graduate? Still at Leicester? You are employed by the Student Union as Deputy President. Is that paid employment?

Murray: No. I have a year's sabbatical leave from my studies.

Stable: You got leave in order to devote yourself full time to being deputy president of the Union. Are you in receipt of a student grant?

Murray: Yes. From the British Government, yes.

Stable: Your branch of the Union is affiliated to NUS?

Murray: Yes.

Stable: Throughouf the time that STST committee was in existence the NUS was one of its affiliated bodies, was it not?

Murray: I have no idea, but I can accept that it was.

Stable: You appreciate that in this country there is freedom to demonstrate in certain circumstances?

Murray: Yes.

Stable: And because of that freedom it is possible for people like you before a demonstration to go to see the police and discuss the matter beforehand and decide on routes and things of that sort. Did you yourself go to the police before the demonstration?

Murray: I did.

Stable: And gave the police to understand that what you were proposing was a lawful peaceful demonstration?

Murray: We told them that we would like to have permission to have a demonstration. We told them the terms of reference of the resolution of the general meeting.

Stable: Did you tell them that a part of the arrangements that you had made at the meeting were that you would support unpeaceful and unlawful demonstrations?

Murray: We never suggested that we would support unpeaceful demonstrations. We did not include the word peaceful.

Stable: I suggest that what you did when you went to the police was that what you proposed was that you wanted to have a peaceful, lawful demonstration?

Murray: I do remember that we discussed the problem of the National Front. We raised the problem with them, and they assured us that they would take care of that, and we came out a lot happier. If we had had a general meeting that afternoon I for one would have moved that the word peaceful be inserted.

Stable: The fact of the matter is that your organisation had decided that it was prepared to support unpeaceful and unlawful demonstrations?

Murray: That was not the fact of the matter. The fact of the matter was that people were not prepared to see their friends or girl friends attacked by people who had already made it clear that they would do everything in their power to stop that demonstration happening. What people understood was that there might be fist fights, etc. In that sense I suppose they realised that they were taking part in something that might be violent.

Stable: Why was it that you were prompted to think by Hain's enthusiasm, 'typical of a bloody Liberal'?

Murray: I know that you don't go with 3,000 people marching down the road, thinking you are going to stop a rugby tour. You don't stop it that way. What you are doing is showing your protest. I knew that there were people inside who were going to take non-violent direct action. But that didn't come off.

Stable: So you knew that apart from your demonstration outside an attempt was being made to get into the ground and there use direct action tactics?

Murray: I had heard vague rumours. I didn't organise that part of it.

Stable: You agree that it was not spontaneous?

Murray: Oh no. 3,000 people at a demonstration has got to be arranged.

Stable: Did you get inside the ground?

Murray: No.

Stable: But you knew people were going to try to get in?

Murray: No. I said people who *were* inside might then use direct non-violent tactics to stop the game.

Judge: How long before the actual match did you know that some persons were going to go into the ground and use non-violent direct methods? On the day of the match or before?

Murray: This was one of the main talking points. You heard all kinds of people come up with all sorts of silly suggestions. But it did seem from the general atmosphere that some people were going to take the protest one stage further and try and stop the match. By the Thursday or Friday before the match it was the topic of conversation. Every day I suppose I heard people say that people should invade the pitch.

Judge: Did you issue any instructions that non-violent direct methods should be taken by anyone in your demonstration?

Murray: We issued instructions asking all students to take part in the demonstration with us. Those were the only instructions we gave.

Stable: Your instructions more or less followed the resolution that had been passed?

Murray: Quite.

Stable: You have told us that your particular role on that demonstration involved remaining outside the ground?

Murray: There were no other roles for people to play that day — that was the role of anyone representing Leicester Students Union.

Stable: Did you go to other matches?

Murray: Manchester and Durham.

Stable: Did you stay outside?

Murray: Yes, on all occasions.

Stable: But you heard that there were those who wished to pursue what you have described as non-violent direct-action tactics?

Murray: Yes.

Stable: What did you mean by non-violent direct-action tactics? Would that, in your opinion, involve getting into the ground?

Murray: No. Not really. It would be a waste of time. All the demonstrations I attended, all the reports I heard, it was extremely difficult to get into the ground without paying. If you mean that buying a ticket with intent to go in and do something is direct action then I accept that.

Stable: You have used the term direct non-violent action. What do you understand by the phrase?

Murray: Action that may possibly be against the law but which involves no injury to persons and that does not damage property in such a way that it can cause damage to people either physical or financial.

Stable: So that what you are really saying is that your understanding is that provided you draw the line at actual physical violence and actual physical damage then anything else goes?

Murray: Yes.

Stable: Whether it is in fact lawful or whether it is unlawful isn't a matter of very great concern to you?

Murray: It is a matter of very great concern. I don't think one should break the law because it is a law, but I think in a democracy that you have to go beyond that sometimes. Morality is above the law.

Stable: What you are really saying is that you are to be the judge as to whether the particular issue is a sufficiently important one or not?

Murray: In the ultimate, yes. And then accept the consequences of that decision.

Stable: If you come to the conclusion that the issue is so important, then morality requires you to break the law if need be?

Murray: Yes.

Stable: Would you agree with me that there are unhappily at the present time a very large number of different issues about which honest and sincere people can feel very strongly?

Murray: Obviously.

Exercising his right of re-examination, Hain probed.

Hain: You said describing the background to the demonstration, that there were these rumours going about. You have also said that as the person concerned with coordinating activities locally those were independent of me. Do you think that the rumours you heard were independent of me?

Murray: Completely. To my knowledge I know the political source from which they came and the last person they would have discussed it with or told or mentioned it to in my opinion would the the Chairman of the Young Liberals.

Hain: You see the problem is that Stable has this grand conspiracy theory. In your experience what is your opinion of that?

Murray: In my opinion, to try to link Leicester with the NUS executive is difficult enough considering our peculiar relations with them; to try to link action taken at Leicester by individuals buying tickets and going into the ground, even to link them with Leicester Students Union is wrong, given the political persuasion of these people.

CHAPTER XI

A man scattering tacks

"I have always been involved politically most of my life. I am a political person."
That was how the next witness introduced himself after giving his particulars — Peter
Jordan, of Bristol, a junior schoolteacher, aged 48 — and telling Hain that they had
neither met or spoken to each other before this moment in court.

"When the South African rugby tour was scheduled to take place I thought it
ought not to take place because of the system of apartheid in South Africa. Most
of my friends and lots of other people I know in Bristol were also opposed to the
tour. I read in the local press that the Young Liberal organisation was trying to
demonstrate against the tour. I attended one or two meetings where Tony Lambert,
local chairman of the Young Liberals, was present. This was once the tour had
started. They were mainly ad hoc meetings where a group of people discussed
what they were going to do about the tour. I was mainly concerned that Bristol
Trades Council should be concerned and on the day of the match it was in fact
the Trades Council that called the march. If it had been suggested that we consult
you or the national STST committee I would have said we don't need advice. We
can organise our own demonstrations and things to do."

Judge Gillis asked Jordan what he understood by "the movement" as referred
to in Hain's book, to which the witness replied that he meant the general feeling
of revulsion against the tour, but if STST was part of that movement then he accepted that. Neither he nor the people in Bristol like him had joined anything, nor
paid any subscription to any organisation, but if people would have agreed at the
time that they were part of the STST movement.

Jordan said the talk in Bristol was of marches with banners, then going onto the
pitches and sitting down, interrupting the game, but he wanted the tour stopped.
"I thought sitting down on a pitch would only stop it for a few minutes and I tried
to conceive some way whereby an actual match could be completely stopped. Having
played a bit of rugby myself, and knowing how the game goes, I thought that if
there was something on the pitch which was dangerous then obviously unless they
could clear it the match wouldn't be able to be played. So I hit on this idea of using
some tacks or something like that with fairly long points and these could be got
onto the pitch."

Stable interrupted this witness' evidence at this point to ask the judge if he should
not warn Jordan that he might be saying things which might incriminate himself.
Judge Gillis gave the warning but as it transpired later there was no point; and the
reason why there was no point in giving the warning was precisely why Hain had
called the man.

"I did not agree with anybody else to do this," he continued. "It was a spontaneous act. I bought a ticket for the Springboks match against Western Counties

on 31 December 1969 and went into the ground carrying several boxes of furniture tacks with long points and some boxes of smaller ones — drawing pins. My intention was to get onto the pitch at some time and scatter the pins on the pitch so that the game would be stopped. I don't mean during the course of the play. If I did that then somebody would get injured, so it had to be before the game started or during half-time. I watched the first half and at half-time I just had to look for the first opportunity to get onto the pitch. There were cordons. I had to keep an eye on the police to see when they weren't watching so that I could nip over and get clear at the best opportunity. I don't think it was apparent to people what I was doing. Whether they thought I was doing a war dance. It was some time before any action happened. Then a policeman came charging up from the other end of the field and got me with a rugby tackle. I had distributed nearly all the tacks before the police got me. A couple of policemen came up and dragged me off the pitch, escorted me to the gates and pushed me outside and told me to go away and not come back. I didn't resist — I was grateful to be getting out. I was walking down the road a couple of minutes later when I met a person I know by sight who said he had been put out of the ground as well. We walked to his car and he got in. I was going to walk on and get a bus when all of a sudden there was a wailing of sirens and a screeching of brakes and a police patrol car came along and they grabbed me. I appeared at Bristol Magistrates' Court on 8 January 1970 charged with breach of the peace and possessing an offensive weapon. I was fined £50 with £5 costs on the weapon charge and agreed to be bound over for twelve months. I don't have any other convictions. The case was widely reported in the press."

Jordan said he was surprised that the match continued becaue he knew how dangerous it was, but he had told the policeman who arrested him what he had done. This was his only act of demonstration during the campaign and it had been, he considered, spontaneous.

Stable: At some time before the Bristol match you had come to the conclusion that disruption of the games by going onto the pitches in a body and sitting down was not sufficiently effective?

Jordan: Yes.

Stable: You wanted something more effective?

Jordan: Yes

Stable: Would I be right in saying that your philosophy is that provided you think that a certain issue is of sufficient importance then what the law permits and what the law forbids is irrelevant?

Jordan: I think that is the philosophy of a lot of people. There are circumstances when it is necessary to stand against the law.

Judge: You are not being asked about standing against the law. Every citizen has a right to protest in a lawful manner against a law he does not support. You are being asked whether if the matter was of sufficient importance in your judgement you would break a law?

Jordan: Yes.

Stable: Prior to this game at Bristol you attended some meetings?

Jordan: Yes.

Stable: How many?

Jordan: Absolutely impossible to say. You can't define the word meeting as an announced place with speakers or a meeting like that. A meeting might be bumping into two or three people in a pub.

Stable: What political organisations did you belong to at that time?

Jordan: I don't see that this has any bearing.

Stable: If I ask you a question which is irrelevant or improper the judge will stop the question being put.

Jordan: Have I got to say?

Judge: Yes. You can refuse to answer any question which —

Jordan: I refuse to answer. I do not consider it relevant or important and I decline to answer.

Judge: You are entitled to decline to answer any question which may incriminate you. You are not entitled not to answer because you don't agree it is important.

Stable: In the winter of 1969 what political organisations did you belong to?

Jordan: None.

Stable: Why then did you tell the jury in your examination-in-chief that you belonged to political organisations?

Jordan: I said I was a political animal.

Stable: When did you last belong to a political organisation? Do you belong to a political organisation at the present time?

Jordan: I do.

Stable: What organisation?

Jordan: I refuse to answer the question.

Stable: In my submission I am entitled to an answer.

Judge: Yes. You are here as a witness. You have made an affirmation. I have ruled that the question is admissable in law. Accordingly it is your duty to answer it.

Hain: Perhaps I could help. It is simply that as far as the defence is concerned Mr. Jordan's political views are irrelevant. If Stable wishes to question him on that I don't mind. The defence doesn't mind.

Judge: It is not for the defence to mind or not or to say whether they are happy or not. When a witness gives evidence in courts in this country he is bound by the rules and procedures of evidence. It is not for a witness to select which questions he regards as proper.

Jordan: Can I have any other further advice?

Judge: You can reserve this question. I shall allow this witness if he wished during the adjournment to seek advice and if he wishes he can return then and make answer.

Stable: I reserve my cross-examination, in that case.

Judge: Counsel may have further cross-examination. If you desire to seek legal advice you should do so. You are not to discuss the evidence you are about to give save with any legal adviser.

For several minutes Jordan consulted with Larry Grant, Hain's solicitor, outside the court. He again climbed into the witness box.

Judge: Have you had an opportunity of obtaining legal advice?

Jordan: Yes.

Judge: What political organisations do you belong to now?

Jordan: I still think this is a kind of McCarthy sort of question. Nevertheless —

Judge: You are not permitted to say anything like that in the witness box.

Jordan: I am giving my answer which is that I am a Communist.

Stable: What political organisation are you now a member of?

Jordan: That is the question I have just answered. I am a member of the national Communist Party.

Stable: When did you join?

Jordan: Early 1970.

Stable: Prior to early 1970 you were not a member of any political organisation?

Jordan: I had been but not for several years.

Stable: What was the last political organisation you belonged to?

Jordan: Also the Communist Party.

Stable: When did you leave it prior to 1970?

Jordan: 1964.

Stable: You told the jury that prior to the match in Bristol you were concerned that Bristol Trades Council ought to become involved in disrupting the match?

Jordan: No. In demonstrating whatever way they thought was effective.

Stable:. Were you, or are you now, a member of the Bristol Trades Council?

Jordan: No.

Stable: How did you give effect to your concern that the Bristol Trades Council become involved?

Jordan: I am a trade unionist. Most of my friends are. I knew people on the Trades Council.

Stable: So you and others lobbied them, that's what it amounts to?

Jordan: That isn't in fact correct. The moves came from other members of the Trades Council. I was giving my support to something they had already decided on.

Stable: What meetings did you attend which were attended by Tony Lambert?

Jordan: I can't remember any meetings. The only one I can remember was a casual meeting in a pub of several people who were — this is something I know, I repeat, the organisation was loose and there were all sorts of people and individuals and groups involved. I can't remember any meeting when he was present apart from a few of us in the pub on one occasion. I can't remember how long before the match it was. I can't remember what was said except in general terms. Probably we talked about what the Trades Council was going to do.

Stable: You in fact said before that you attended some meetings at which he was present.

Jordan: I am sure he was present on other occasions. This is why I didn't try to tie it down. I can only remember one occasion specifically.

Stable: About how many gatherings do you think there were prior to this match which you attended or formed part of at which you discussed tactics to be employed to prevent or disrupt the match?

Jordan: I don't remember whether a meeting to discuss tactics ever took place. If you mean, well are we going to have a demonstration or are we going to sit down on the pitch this was talked about all the time. There was no specific meeting I attended which was called to discuss tactics on the day of the match.

Stable: Were you aware that the Young Communist League was part and parcel of STST?

Jordan: I was not aware, but I am not surprised.

Stable: At these various meetings or gatherings were there people of different political persuasions or were they all members of the Communist Party and sympathisers?

Jordan: I have no idea. I wasn't concerned to ask. I know that there were other Communist Party members involved, I know Labour Party was involved, I know the Liberal Party was involved. But apart from one or two people I knew I have no idea. Nobody asked.

Stable: At these meetings did you consider and discuss what had been done elsewhere in relation to preventing and disrupting the tour?

Jordan: They talked about what had happened on previous matches.

Stable: Were you aware of STST working to disrupt the tour?

Jordan: I knew there was an STST campaign.

Stable: And that it was working to disrupt the tour?

Hain: Could Stable say what he means by 'working to disrupt the tour' so that the witness can answer?

Stable: You knew of STST. Did you know which tour was referred to in that title?

Jordan: The cricket tour.

Stable: Did you also know that that same organisation was concerning itself with the rugby tour?

Jordan: Yes.

Stable: Did you know that it was co-ordinating all groups to disrupt matches?

Jordan: No, I did not.

Stable: If you knew that it was also concerning itself to stop the rugby tour or disrupt games did you know how it was setting about those plans?

Jordan: All I knew was what I read in the press. As far as I remember it was a campaign, an organisation which was protesting against the tour. That was as much as I knew.

Stable: Did you know that it was primarily organising mass demonstrations onto the pitch during play?

Jordan: I did know.

Stable: Did you also know that it was organising the hounding of the players wherever they happened to go or be?

Jordan: No.

Stable: At these meetings was there any discussion about this organisation?

Jordan: Not as far as I remember. We were completely local individual people. Not organised in any single organisation at all.

Hain: We have had an entertaining tour through your political views.

Stable: I have asked no questions about his political views. I only asked him what political organisations he belonged to.

Judge: It is not for counsel (or you defending yourself) to comment on the evidence of witnesses during cross-examination.

CHAPTER XII

The Black View

The first Black into the witness box, Jeff Crawford, who had been secretary of the West Indian Standing Conference from 1963 to 1970, explained why the West Indian community in Britain had taken little part in the rugby campaign. "Rugby is rather alien to West Indians and we thought it better to wait for the cricket tour", he said. He had been involved in similar protests before — in 1967 his organisation had sent 30,000 leaflets by boat from England to Barbados protesting against the inclusion of two white South Africans and one white Rhodesian in an international game in Bridgetown. "We felt in 1969 most affronted at the very thought of issuing such an invitation to an all-white team which was a racial one. There was no doubt in my mind, and in the minds of my Black brothers and sisters in this country, that this would have led to a substantial deterioration of race relations in this country and have caused reactions in the Caribbean and throughout the world. Since we are concerned with racial troubles between black and white we felt we had to do something about it. Not only to save ourselves but to save the human race.

"In February 1970 I helped form the West Indian Campaign against Apartheid Cricket with a membership far wider than the West Indian Standing Conference. All sections of opinion came together, from politicians to preachers. It was formed independent of Hain but we knew that other people were making plans to try to stop the tour and since STST happened to be one of the groups I decided to contact it. There was no question of merging but as we were working towards similar objectives there would be some degree of co-ordination. We had our own policy committee and we made our decision on our own.

"I organised a protest at Lords and at the Oval to highlight to the public our feelings of what would inevitably happen if the tour was not cancelled. In addition to writing to the MCC I wrote on behalf of the Campaign an individual letter to all West Indian and Asian cricketers that we knew of pointing out what we considered to be their moral obligation to us and the community at large to say where they stood and the dangers that would follow if the tour took place, and urged them to refuse to support such a racialist policy. We cabled the West Indian Board of Cricket Control telling them of our concern and asked them to follow Indian and Pakistan's example of advising players not to play against the South Africans."

Crawford said his campaign was non-violent and that was why he cooperated with STST because he had heard Hain say publicly and privately that he was against violence and damage to property. He was also on the Fair Cricket Campaign, set up by the Reverend David Sheppard, Bishop of Woolwich. While Hain was probing for Crawford's view of the racial situation in Britain at the time and how the 1970 tour might have affected it, Stable objected that the witness could not know the answer to some of these questions. Judge Gillis took the opportunity to lecture Hain on the state of the case as he saw it.

"Some of your questions are going a little bit beyond the proper province", he told Hain. "You must understand what the issues in this trial are. It is not that there was not a vast body of opinion throughout the world which would wish to have stopped the tour and thought that for the tour to continue would lead or might lead to unrest or the aggravation of grave social problems. What the jury have to consider is whether the acts complained of were done. In this country the rule of law is supreme. And the rights of every person to go about his lawful occasions in a lawful manner are secure. And no one has the right to say to any such person, I don't agree with what you are doing and I shall not tolerate it. A word I think which fell from the lips of Murray. If you disagree you are fully entitled to protest personally and fully entitled to ask groups to join your protest provided the law of the land is not broken. And so I hesitate to stop you, but I am getting anxious to see what the effect is of some of your questions. Undoubtedly there was a vast body of opinion against the holding of the tour. On the other hand other persons may have had different views. And as long as they confine themselves to doing it lawfully they are as much entitled to exercise their rights as you are to protest. To deny to others the freedom a demonstrator claims for himself is to invade his own personal rights. It seems to me that you are going beyond what are the strict issues of fact."

Hain: I am particularly concerned here with the fourth count where it is alleged that I conspired to threaten to stop the cricket tour. The relevance of my submission is this: Crawford has given evidence to the extent that he as a West Indian was opposed to the tour. That he organised with other West Indians in opposition to the tour, and that he did so independently of me. I think it is vital for the jury and to your view of what my role might have been in this cancellation.

Judge: Certainly. But it is not the case for the prosecution that the demonstrating was confined to you and those alleged to be acting with you. The prosecution made that clear. The fact that there may have been a million other persons is not relevant to the issues. It seemed to me that you were not appreciating that during some of your questions.

Hain: I am concerned to establish that there was no nationwide conspiracy and Stable said it was at the heart of the prosecution case that there was. If I can show that there was no such conspiracy, indeed if the jury are satisfied that in the context which preceeded the tour it was not possible to have any such conspiracy because so many people were acting alone then they are in a position to view my role and my alleged offences in a much sounder light.

Judge: The jury will find their verdict on the evidence before them. On that evidence the prosecution will have to convince the jury that you were party, whatever the evidence may show or may not show in relation to any other persons. That is the narrow and limited area.

Hain: That is the area on which I will be found guilty or not guilty. But what I am submitting is that in order to judge — in a very difficult area of the law — events which took place the whole length and breadth of the country — I am alleged to have agreed in over 200 particulars. Returning to the ruling of the narrow issue at stake, the jury may decide that not only did I not conspire but to suggest that there was a conspiracy in view of the matters Crawford and others have described would be ridiculous.

Judge: That point you make through your submission. What you must be clear about is the precise and limited nature of the charges. If the jury came to the conclusion that to describe a nationwide conspiracy was the language of exaggeration that is not the end of the case. They may well find that whatever language counsel use to describe the activities there is evidence to prove that you were party to the matter complained of. You must not confuse allegations of nationwide conspiracy and the precise charges the jury have to give their judgement on.

Hain: I am seeking to clarify rather than confuse it.

Stable: I might clarify this. Although I did speak of nationwide conspiracy it certainly isn't my case that there was a nationwide conspiracy in relation to Counts 2 and 3 of the indictment. My submission to the jury in relation to Count 3 was that the conspirators were probably only three or four people and that in relation to the Wilf Isaac XI, though the conspiracy was somewhat larger, it was a very small matter.

Hain: You would have run non-violently onto a pitch?

Crawford: Yes.

Judge: How would you have done that when you come from the spectators and the police are guarding the pitch? By nipping out when they weren't noticing or slipping past?

Crawford: Yes.

Judge: Are you confusing physical violence with unlawful actions?

Crawford: I certainly wouldn't knock a policeman down intentionally.

Judge: But to go on the pitch non-violently, you mean unlawfully, don't you?

Crawford: I take it you are implying that to go onto a pitch is an unlawful act? Perhaps I would like your guidance.

Judge: In my view of the law of England it is trespassing. Done by a number of persons it would be a conspiracy to trespass tryable by a jury.

Crawford: In retrospect, I would have run onto the pitch.

Hain: You described feeling in the black community as high?

Crawford: Yes.

Hain: Would you feel to your knowledge that other black people would have done the same as you?

Crawford: Oh certainly. As I said earlier we were approached by a number of people and encouraged to do something by way of an organised campaign against the tour.

Hain had written in his book (p. 172) of Crawford contacting him: "We met and discussed the whole issue of the tour and what role West Indians could play in the campaign." Stable's cross-examination of the West Indian witness was confined almost entirely to trying to establish whether this meeting was conspiratorial. Crawford fenced the skilled lawyer as best he could and the Judge pressed him to bring his mind back to this meeting but Crawford stuck to his attitude that the discussion was 'vague and general'.

Stable: I want you to try and concentrate your mind. You are going to talk of the role West Indians could play in the campaign. You said before, "how could West Indians be fitted into the campaign". The campaign was the one Hain was planning to run through STST. That's right, isn't it? You have agreed that you discussed the whole issue of the tour and what role West Indians could play. You yourself used the words, "how West Indians could be fitted into the campaign".

Crawford: I thought I said how we could fit in; where it was possible for us to work together. I am not suggesting that we said we want to become full part of STST — perhaps "fit in" was a bad choice of words —

Stable: No, no. I am not suggesting for a moment that you suggested merging. What you were trying to explore with Hain were what his plans were and how you could best, with the support you represented, best assist in those plans?

Crawford: Not "assist" at all. How we could work together.

Judge: By "we" you mean the West Indian organisation you were representing?

Crawford: Yes.

Judge: With whom were you trying to find out how you could work together? STST?

Crawford: We were independent and we stayed independent. We were primarily concerned with areas of coordination.

Stable: Did you at that meeting agree with Hain that you would work in conjunction — in coordination — with him in relation to the tour?

Crawford: It wasn't a question of Jeff Crawford working with Peter Hain at all.

Stable: No. But it was getting your people to work in with, and coordinate with, STST?

Crawford: Where and when agreed we would work together as two independent bodies agreeing to work together.

Stable: Yes. Subject to an agreement being reached between the two bodies?

Crawford: I don't want any confusion about there being a literal agreement to work together.

Stable: Let's take it a little further. From that first meeting you did work fairly close with that campaign?

Crawford: Yes. We were the two men empowered to act in the name of the bodies.

Stable: Peter Hain was clearly the head of what STST represented, and you were the head of the West Indian Campaign against Apartheid Cricket?

Crawford: Well in a very generalised manner, in that we were the two men empowered to act on behalf of and in the name of rather than the two lawmakers.

Stable: You told us in your evidence that had the tour gone on, you would have continued with your plans. You went on, "I would have run onto the pitches, that was one of the things we had decided upon".

Crawford: Yes, the "we" referred to the West Indian Campaign.

Stable: Did you ask at this meeting in fact what it was Mr. Hain was planning to do?

Crawford: I discussed with Mr. Hain what others were planning to do. I never dealt with Mr. Hain just as an individual.

Stable: I accept that you as leader of the West Indian campaign against apartheid cricket were speaking to Mr. Hain in that capacity and you understood that Mr. Hain was acting as the information officer of STST?

Crawford: More or less, yes.

Stable: I will frame my question differently. Did Mr. Hain as information officer of STST tell you what STST were planning to do if the tour took place?

Crawford: Naturally, yes, we discussed what should happen then and what could have happened.

Stable: When he was telling you of the plans of STST if the tour took place, did he tell you that it was part of their plans to go onto the pitches in numbers during play?

Crawford: Yes, this was mentioned. This was one of the possible methods.

Stable: Having gone onto the pitches in numbers, were the people who had gone onto the pitches to sit down or otherwise remain there?

Crawford: Yes.

Stable: Did he tell you that during the rugby tour dye had been thrown onto the ground?

Crawford: No, you will recollect that we didn't go into detail.

Stable: Did he tell you that smoke cannisters had been thrown onto the ground?

Crawford: On what occasion?

Stable: I am asking you whether at the meeting in February, whether Mr. Hain told you that during the rugby tour, whether he told you that cannisters had been thrown onto the pitches.

Crawford: I can only repeat that we didn't discuss it.

Stable: Did he tell you that during the rugby tour tin tacks and nails had been thrown onto the pitches?

Crawford: No.

Stable: Did he tell you that he wanted to try and stop the tour before it began rather than it being stopped in the middle after it had begun?

Crawford: Yes, this was a general hope.

Stable: Did he tell you how he hoped to achieve that?

Crawford: I don't recollect that we were very detailed. It is possible that we did in a general way discuss how the tour might be stopped.

Stable: Would I be right in saying that at that meeting you envisaged that if you were, that there would be police present at cricket matches, whose duty it would be to try and stop you getting onto pitches?

Crawford: That was envisaged.

Stable: Would I be right in thinking that the fact that the police were there to stop people going onto the pitches in numbers was not a matter which you considered crucial in deciding whether you would go forward with your plans or not?

Crawford: Yes.

Stable: It was obvious to you that if there were such police present, that would be the reason they were there?

Crawford: Yes.

Stable: It was part of your plans to go onto the pitches notwithstanding the presence of police to prevent you?

Crawford: Yes.

Stable: Did Mr. Hain tell you that it was part of his plan to follow the players about?

Crawford: I don't recollect that being mentioned.

Stable: Were you aware that a few days before you met Mr. Hain a large number of cricket grounds had been damaged?

Crawford: I am not sure about the sequence here.

Stable: I can tell you that on the night of 19 January a number of cricket grounds were damaged and you were meeting Mr. Hain early in February, so were you aware?

Crawford: Oh yes, I was fully aware of what had been going on, because I was part of what was going on because I was concerned and involved.
Stable: Did you discuss it with Mr. Hain at that meeting?
Crawford: It was at that meeting or a subsequent one that this would have been mentioned, but only by the way of whether we should draw the line at this sort of thing — wilful and unlawful damage.

Crawford was asked by Stable about his part in the STST conference at Hampstead Town Hall on 7 March 1970. He was a speaker along with Hain, Mike Craft, an STST official, Mike Brearley, the Middlesex County cricket captain, and Professor John Rex. Crawford agreed that Brearley, while opposed to the tour taking place, did not accept non-violent direct action tactics. On the subject of his letter to all Black cricketers playing for county clubs in England, Stable asked him if it had been his intention to persuade them to break their contracts of employment, to which Crawford replied: "If we had succeeded, yes, but at that stage we were asking them to do their bit by standing down". He didn't know of any who disagreed although some did not reply. Asked about Basil D'Oliveira's view that the tour should go on, Crawford said he regarded it as an honest but irrational attitude. During one of the longest cross-examinations of the trial, Crawford played a dead-bat to Stable's probing as to how much he was under the influence and guidance of Hain until an exasperated Stable remarked: "I suspect you are highly intelligent. I ask you questions and you go off at a tangent without answering the question." Crawford agreed that the West Indians had discussed withdrawing their labour from London Transport on 6 June 1970 unless the tour was cancelled and black-listing of any West Indian who played against the South Africans. They had not decided what blacklisting would involve.

*   *   *

A British-born Black, 23-year old Harry Joshua, who told the court he was a part-time lecturer with the extramural department of the University in Cardiff, described how in 1969 when he was a student and chairman of the Third World Society they called a meeting in connection with the proposed Springbok rugby tour. They had as speaker Dennis Brutus, secretary of the South African Non-Racial Olympic Committee (SAN-ROC). As a result a committee called Wales Rejects Apartheid was formed, representing students of South Wales, Bristol, Newport and other parts of Wales, representatives of the Labour Party, the Communist Party, the church and the trade unions, particularly the miners' union. He was elected secretary.

The committee was advertised in the local paper, the *Western Mail,* and the cost met by people ranging from poets to miners, solicitors to university lecturers. The Wales Rejects Apartheid Committee aided the organisation of the match at Newport at which 700 demonstrated, which passed off peacefully, and for three coachloads of people to go from Cardiff to demonstrate at the Swansea match on 15 November. He had not consulted the STST committee in London before doing so. Joshua's description of what happened is an interesting comparison with Wooller's.

"The demonstration began in the centre of town", he said, "and marched towards the Swansea rugby pitch. I think it is significant that the police preconceived a situation where violence was almost inevitable because there were approximately 1,000 demonstrators and there were exactly 1,000 policemen. I have not come across any instances where you need one policeman per demonstrator to control the crowd. Outside the rugby pitch the police attempted to contain the demonstration on one side of the road and attacks were made by vigilantes both inside, and to my knowledge, outside the ground. And I think there was general hysteria on the part of the police because the demonstration set out to be a peaceful demonstration. I am saying that the demonstration set out to be peaceful and violence only resulted in the demonstration when the police forced the entire demonstration against a wall and the police were forcing the demonstrators into the wall and into the sea. It was inevitable that violence would emerge. Our committee had specifically said that it was its purpose to organise peaceful demonstrations. There was no contact with STST about the planning of the demonstration."

Joshua told the jury that they sent coaches to the Springboks matches at Ebbw Vale, and prior to the Cardiff match they organised a public meeting addressed by Michael Foot, MP, Glyn Davies, the Olympic long-jumper, the Archbishop of Monmouthshire and the secretary of the National Union of Miners. Precious McKenzie, the former South African weight lifter, was also on the platform. The black community in Tiger Bay held a protest meeting against the rugby tour, addressed by the African National Congress. Black people threatened to withhold a week's rent if the Cardiff City Council carried out its intention of entertaining the South African tourists. There was a general opposition and they leafleted factories, schools, trade unions. At this stage they had no contact with STST.

The Cardiff demonstration was entirely peaceful despite all the talk of violence, and he and others went into the ground and shouted slogans. A fire had started in some straw bales near the stand and a number of rugby supporters assumed it had been started by them — in fact they had nothing to do with the fire, said Joshua — and moved close. "One threw a punch which started a fight with the demonstrators in general. As soon as the fracas started several constables leapt out and arrested three of the demonstrators including myself. I was charged with causing a breach of the peace but was acquitted in court." Joshua described the nature of the opposition for the second Springboks match at Cardiff on 24 January 1970: "I would say two-thirds townspeople and people from the valleys and one-third students and black people from the local area. It was a peaceful march, organised by our committee, and there were no arrests."

Joshua said he was aware that a group from Bangor University and another from Cardiff University, with help from some members of the Labour Party planned to disrupt the match. The point that all the actions of the demonstrators in Wales was quite independent of him was being made frequently by Hain in his attempt to smash the 'nationwide conspiracy' allegation by the prosecution. No one, let alone Hain, from outside of Wales had organised their demonstrations, said Joshua.

When he rose to cross-examine Joshua, Stable came immediately to the point of the involvement of Dennis Brutus in the Welsh campaign. Did he know that Brutus was closely involved in the activities of STST? Joshua said he didn't know. He knew him as the president of SAN-ROC and very prominent in the Anti-Apartheid Movement.

Stable: Was it Mr. Brutus who suggested to you at the very inception that the best way of forming an organisation was to have, as it were, a two-faced organisation, one centred on legal activities so that you could get people like the Archbishop of Wales to support it, and the other face where you centred on unlawful methods so as to be more effective?

Joshua: There are two answers. First of all, Mr. Brutus didn't suggest that and I was not aware that anyone was organising unlawful activity.

Stable: Can you repeat what you said?

Joshua: I am using your terms. I said that I, at the time, was in close touch with, I was not organising.

Judge: You said you were organising demonstrations, etc., and were in close touch with other people who were not intending to maintain the protests on a lawful level.

Stable: What do you mean by "in close touch with"? Were you coordinating your activities with theirs?

Joshua: No.

Stable: Were you finding out what their plans were?

Joshua: Yes.

Stable: Their plans were for what has been described as direct action tactics, that is right isn't it?

Joshua: You will have to explain to me what direct action tactics are before I can agree.

Stable: I will certainly do that. (The prosecutor then referred the witness to pages 124, 148 and 200 of Hains' book.)

Joshua: It would be correct to say that direct action tactics as far as the locality of South Wales is concerned would include the invasion of fields.

Stable: Did direct action tactics, having shown you what Mr. Hain defines as direct action tactics, are you saying that in South Wales direct action tactics go further?

Joshua: Further in what sense?

Stable: Further in the sense of not merely confining it to sitting down and invading pitches, obstruction of coach journeys, etc?

Joshua: Direct action as far as I am aware would include invasion of the fields, sit-downs, but it would not involve obstructing coach journeys.

CHAPTER XIII

Trespassers were not prosecuted

Up to this point the trial had taken a fairly normal course, even with Hain, the amateur lawyer, conducting his own defence. The judge had to rebuke him only occasionally for accidentally putting a leading question to a witness. But from the moment the Bishop of Stepney, Trevor Huddleston stepped into the witness box at 10.55 am on 8 August the whole atmosphere of the trial changed. Stable was quick to show his resentment of the introduction of 'big names' despite his own liberal use of them. The prosecution's heavyweights were famous in sporting circles; the defence's answer was people with moral and political standing. No sooner had the Bishop of Stepney given his name and home address when Stable lodged his first objection. Hain had asked the Bishop where he was educated – Lancing, was the reply.

Stable: I cannot see the relevance of this, my Lordship, it is inadmissable.
Hain: Your Lordship, in the prosecution we hear of Mr. Isaac's sporting background, educational background –
Judge: Not his educational background.
Hain: The idea of this question was to introduce him to the court.

Questions about the Bishop's theological training and ordainment went uninterrupted. When he spoke of his religious order Stable was again quickly on his feet.

Stable: My Lord, I object to this. My objection is that whatever community Father Huddleston is a member of has no relevance in this case.
Hain: I was under the impression that if a group or institution was mentioned, the witness had to explain it to the court.
Judge: The jury are only concerned with the evidence given here. Kindly put your next question, Mr. Hain.
Hain: Certainly, my Lordship. In 1954, did you write an article in the *Observer*?
Bishop: Yes, I did.
Stable: My Lord, I object to that question. I cannot see whether it matters two hoots what he wrote in 1954.
Hain: My next question to Bishop Huddleston would have been what he did in 1969/70. He did not just arrive on the scene, I wish the court to understand the background to his involvement.
Stable: I cannot explain to Mr. Hain the relevance of Mr. Isaac's evidence, he was giving evidence that he had been spat upon, called a racist bum. This had been his view and so it was relevant.
Judge: The reference you gave to Mr. Isaacs indicates the difficulty in which you are in and you do not understand the legal distinctions.
Hain: Very well, your Lordship. I still have a lot of evidence to get from Bishop Huddleston.

Judge: I am willing to hear, Mr. Hain, but I warn you that I shall have to stop you as my duty as presiding judge, though I shall assist you as much as I can.

Hain: I am grateful to you, my Lordship. I will move on to ask of him his involvement in the 1969/70 campaign. Can you recall in 1969/70 the rugby tour, the South African rugby tour and what your major activity was?

Stable: My Lord, again I object to this question. I have given some thought to this matter. I have not objected up to now, but what Mr. Hain seems to be doing is to avoid the issues which are before the jury. He seems to be trying to set up issues which are not before the jury. 1 — was there an agreement between two or more people to do what is alleged in the indictment? 2 — Was Mr. Hain a party to it? 3 — Did the agreement in question refer to unlawful means of achieving this object? And those are the issues which he has to meet. Mr. Hain is calling people who feel strongly about apartheid, or calling people who have no connections with Mr. Hain. In my submission it is not coming any nearer towards those issues. The evidence merely proves that the particular witness was not party to any of the agreements that Mr. Hain was party to.

Hain: This last sentence begs the question. How can the court know that Bishop Huddleston had not agreed, conspired with me, etc? It does not know because it has not heard the evidence. Yesterday, we had the witness Mr. Joshua. I am accused of conspiring to throw tacks onto the pitch, we also had a witness who ran onto the pitch, I am also accused of conspiring to do this. I cannot see how Mr. Stable's objection can be upheld.

Stable: What Mr. Hain has got to meet is the part that he has played. If the Bishop's evidence is that he was closely associated with Mr. Hain that merely goes to prove that the Bishop joined the conspiracy. But it does not go to prove that Mr. Hain did not. Even if Bishop Huddleston said he was concerned but did it independently it does not affect the issue.

Judge: During yesterday when I was listening to the evidence it seemed to me that much of the evidence given by the witnesses was not strictly relevant to the case. Though all mentioned their deeply felt views on apartheid and that they did not do anything in association with the defendant. The defendant seems to have called witnesses to study their views on apartheid and what they do in objection to apartheid.

Hain: I wish to proceed and ask Bishop Huddleston about his participation in demonstrations with me. Did you attend a demonstration at Twickenham rugby ground on 20 December 1969?

Bishop: I would not be certain of the day.

Hain: Was I present with you at that demonstration?

Bishop: I cannot really remember. It is hard to remember who was with me.

Hain: Had you met me and my family before?

Bishop: Yes.

Hain: What impression as to non-violence did you gain from those meetings?

Bishop: I would not support anybody who was advocating violence against the person and I never got the impression at any time that you were advocating violence in that sense.

Hain: On that point, Bishop Huddleston, do you believe in non-violent direct action?

Stable: That is not a question.

98

Hain: Your Lordship, the term direct action has cropped up time and again in this case. I seek to ask the same question to Bishop Huddleston.
Judge: You are suffering again from lack of legal knowledge, Mr. Hain. The opinion of this witness is no more admissable than five hundred people sitting on the embankment listening to a concert.
Hain: May I refer you to the indictment. I am doing my best to come to terms with the charges brought against me.
Judge: I appreciate that you are doing your best, Mr. Hain, but I pointed out the burden you were taking on yourself. Do not make speeches. You will have ample time to address the jury at the end.
Hain: Your Lordship, thank you. May I refer to Count 1 and 4 on the indictment. I am accused of conspiracy to hinder and disrupt and, on Count 4, "by continually insulting", etc. On these two counts there was "a national conspiracy" and so never alleged in specific terms. I am faced with the difficulty of coming to terms with this. Organisations throughout the country acted independently of me and I have shown this by a number of witnesses.
Judge: You have certainly done that, but there is evidence in your book of this too. The duties of the judge are to prevent unnecessary repetition.
Hain: I really do want to make the point that I am seeking, and it has been prepared over the weeks to bring witnesses to show that they either did things on their own accord and that is one of the major parts of my defence. The book does not indicate a conspiracy by me.
Judge: Mr. Hain, you are not permitted to ask the witnesses' opinion.
Hain: I am endeavouring to ask this witness what he did and whether he did it in agreement with me and this is what I am seeking to do. Bishop Huddleston, did you ever hear me —
Stable: I ought to point out that the question was, "what is your opinion of non-violence?".
Hain: Do you recall any occasion when I was present when I advocated non-violent direct action?
Bishop: I do not recall any terms I can quote from. I assumed that the activities you were involved in were non-violent. I have been involved in demonstrations for years.

Hain tried several more questions to Bishop Huddleston in an attempt to bring out his connections with the anti-cricket tour campaign and his views on apartheid and the use of non-violent direct action. Lacking the necessary legal guile to phrase his questions, the judge and Stable jumped on him each time and the Bishop's evidence stuttered to an embarrassing end a few minutes later. The final question, nevertheless, hit the nail on the head so far as the Bishop was concerned.

Hain: In an interview in the *Times* on 29 April 1970 did you say you would support any of your clergymen who invaded pitches non-violently?
Bishop: They would have my support.
Hain: Would this include invasion of pitches?
Bishop: I would not call invasion of pitches violent.

The trial swerved back onto course on the arrival of the next witness, Anthony John Kitchener, an Oxford journalist, who said he had been secretary of the Oxford branch of the Communist Party of Great Britain since November, 1968. In June of 1969 the branch committee discussed the Wilf Isaacs cricket match due in the town the next month. "We decided to dig up the pitch, send leaflets to people in the town calling them to protest and organise two demonstrations against the match", he said. "The pitch was dug up on 7 July, a Saturday, before the game started, and we gave out the pamphlets. I do not know who dug up the pitch. At 4 pm on the day of the game I went to the ground and after the tea interval there was a sit-down demonstration on the pitch. I blew one of the whistles, but I did not agree with Hain to do so. I had never met him. About 80 people were on the pitches, some making speeches. Police arrested four people when we refused to move but after discussion they agreed to release them if we would all go off peacefully. There was no violence. The aim of the demonstration was to make an orderly protest against the playing of the game and of the tour itself. I don't think any mirrors were used on the pitch and I was not paid by the BBC, or Labour, Liberal or Communist parties to demonstrate. Nobody took any drugs. The demonstration had nothing to do with the Young Liberals.

"When the Springbok rugby tour was due to start we formed a so-called Fireworks Day Committee which originally was townspeople, trade unionists and other individuals interested in the anti-apartheid movement. Its purpose was to build up support for the march and to arrange a demonstration in Oxford. I was secretary of the Fireworks Day Committee and I had no contact with Hain except that I was on the mailing list of STST. In Oxford STST played very little part. Not much really. We didn't receive STST's leaflets: we printed our own."

Kitchener's evidence was damaging to the prosecution case because he had said that a committee had decided to dig the pitch to stop the Wilf Isaacs game, and a link with Hain had not been shown. Answering Stable's cross-examination, Kitchener said ten or eleven members of the local Communist Party had made the decision and he agreed that the action was an unlawful thing to do.

Stable: Was that part of what you described to the jury as an orderly protest against the match?

Kitchener: No. I was referring to the demonstration.

Stable: Having started your protest like that, your protest was criminal throughout?

Kitchener: No.

Stable: You know and well, do you not, that you have no lawful right to go onto the ground of a cricket pitch in this country en masse and sit down on it and interrupt play?

Kitchener: Is there a law against it? What sort of offence are you committing?

Stable: Mass trespass in numbers is unlawful.

Kitchener: Not one of those people were charged with trespassing.

Stable: You thought you had a lawful right to go on 80 strong onto the ground of a cricket match?

Kitchener: I think this is a confused issue which is not clear in law.

Judge: A number of persons agreeing to enter a place to which they have no lawful right in my view is unlawful. The offence is the conspiracy of this.

Stable probed the witness as to whether he considered they had been a local action group or a regional centre, to which Kitchener answered it was the former. He was not aware that there were any regional centres, although he knew there was a committee and he received circulars from it.

Stable: I suggest these local groups, of which you were one, were trying to co-ordinate your activities and, as it were, Manchester would ring up Oxford and ask what your plans were?
Kitchener: We had arranged a peaceful demonstration which we had announced and we were asked about the time and place of the demonstration. We did not send information, except when we were asked.
Stable: That was the object of the national committee, was it not?
Kitchener: No, I don't think so.

It was becoming clear from the length of Stable's cross-examinations of witnesses for the defence that he hoped to get them to confirm the conspiracy theory. The only evidence of this that the prosecution had presented during its case were extracts from the book, which Hain was contending could be read two different ways. Hain had said at the opening of his defence case that he could have called 50,000 witnesses. A good many were lined up in the corridor outside the court or warned to be ready to come to court. That night Hain and his defence advisers met to select only those witnesses who could stand up to Stable's piercing cross-examinations: two of them were women.

Maureen Baker, married to a university lecturer, with three children, a part-time lecturer herself, described next day to the jury how she was elected secretary of the Leeds STST group in February 1970. At the same time she was secretary of the Congress of Racial Equality. A public meeting was called in Leeds at which Abdul Minty, secretary of the Anti-Apartheid Movement, and Peter Hain, chairman of STST, were asked to speak. "Hain advocated non-violent direct action, peaceful approaches", she said. "At the end of the meeting questions were directed at Hain as to what he meant by non-violent direct action, and he specifically replied that it meant avoid damage to property or injury to persons. Hain was against digging up cricket pitches because it was counter-productive. The Leeds STST group ordered leaflets and posters from the national organisation but acted independently of it, just as they did with AAM."

Stable then began a lengthy cross-examination, asking which documents the Leeds group had ordered from national STST and what advice the leaflets had given to demonstrators, such as seizing the cricket ball and keeping it so that the new ball would have to be scraped down to make it similar to the lost one. Mrs. Baker thought this was a pretty poor idea as a disruptive tactic. She agreed with Stable that the Leeds STST group took in the whole of Yorkshire as its territory, and that meant two cricket grounds, Leeds and Sheffield, on which the Springboks would play and which they intended to disrupt. "We all felt, and I still feel, we acted within the law", said Mrs. Baker.

Hain's tactics were to call as witnesses people who could say that they had, quite independently of him, done or planned such-and-such an act of protest against one of the South African sporting tours. But neither the prosecution nor the judge wanted to allow this, but unknown to the judge the evidence of these witnesses had been approved by his legal advisers and Sherrard and Capstick. It was one of the major disadvantages of Hain defending himself that he could not cite chapter and verse authority for calling such evidence whereas Sherrard would have the expertise to frame his questions so as to comply with legal rules and the knowledge of decided cases which authorised the calling of this evidence. Hain was unable to fight in these murky legal waters. Objections from the prosecution came thick and fast at this stage of the trial, and the best example is this one when a research student, Julian Fulbrook, of Cambridge, was giving evidence about his part in the protest movement mounted at Exeter University in 1969.

Hain: Were you aware that the South African rugby team was due to play Devon and Cornwall on December 6th 1969?

Fulbrook: Yes, it had been in the local press for some time.

Hain: Did you decide with another person to take action regarding this match?

Fulbrook: Yes, after a great deal of discussion my friend and I decided we would take some action over and above a peaceful demonstration. We decided between ourselves that this was the way we should aid the Anti-Apartheid group. I, with my friend, decided in fact that we ought to go further than this, privately and individually.

Hain: What did you do, Mr. Fulbrook?

Stable: My Lord, again to remind you that we are not concerned whether Mr. Fulbrook with his friend in Devonshire decided to go over and above a peaceful demonstration outside the ground by doing something unlawful. We are concerned in whether Mr. Hain was party to a confederation to pursue and incite their object by unlawful means. That is the issue which Mr. Hain will not face.

Judge: Mr. Hain, this is just another matter which I had to bring to your attention yesterday. It is not an issue before the jury unless he can give evidence about your conduct. You called a witness. The witness can only give evidence of what is permissable in law. You must not seek to put questions which are not permissable in law.

Hain: As it relates to Count 1, clause 6, where I am accused of conspiring with others unknown between a long period over the whole of the country to commit unlawful and malicious damage, if I can show not only through my book that I did not do that, but in addition call many other people who did spontaneously of their own accord, then I believe I have proved I am not guilty.

Judge: You are not entitled to call evidence which is irrelevant. Other people's conduct is irrelevant. If you would call the whole of the population of Devonshire to say what they did by way of protest that would not exclude the prosecution too. You are failing to concentrate on what I made abundantly clear to you. If this witness or any other witness can speak of your conduct then that evidence would appear to be wholly relevant. They cannot speak as to their conduct because what others may have done is not an answer to what the prosecution may prove you have done. The evidence of the prosecution should be relied on against you, and that is described in your own admittance contained in your own book. I cannot allow further repetition of what is an attempt in my view now to go beyond what you must realise can be permitted.

Hain: In addition to the book Mr. Stable called evidence. He called a number of witnesses and called the captain of the team involved in the rugby tour, and additional evidence was given of facts of that tour beyond the book.

Judge: Perfectly permissable evidence. No objection being taken by your learned counsel, because it is in regard to those tours, those occasions when the prosecution complained about you and therefore their witnesses spoke to their occasion.

Hain: Your Lordship, if I am charged with a certain crime, can I not be allowed to call a man to say that he committed the same crime?

Judge Gillis allowed Hain to ask the witness what, in relation to the demonstration organised at Exeter, he did. Fulbrook replied that as well as organising the peaceful protest outside the ground on the day of the match, a friend and he went into the pitch late at night and painted a sign on the grass near the main stand. He was not actually at the demonstration because he had to go to Cambridge. He had had nothing to do with the group who went into the team's hotel at Exeter on the night before the game and did not know about it until he read an account in the newspapers.

CHAPTER XIV

Enter the Secret Police

The longest witness of the whole trial was Ethel de Keyser, a South African living in London, who had been executive secretary of the Anti-Apartheid Movement for 13 years. AAM was a member of STST and she was also an executive member of the Fair Cricket Campaign during its existence.

Mrs. de Keyser had barely begun her evidence when Hain upset the legal apple cart yet again by his too-blunt approach. He asked her if one of AAM's 45 branches took an illegal course of action on anti-apartheid, would she feel responsible? Stable jumped up to say that the lady's feelings were wholly irrelevant and the judge said Mrs. de Keyser was not required to answer the question. Hain protested that some of the earlier defence witnesses had been asked by the prosecution if they were members of local AAM branches, thereby showing a link with him, and all he wished to do was show the reality of the situation. Stable graciously showed Hain how to put the question.

Stable: Ask Mrs. de Keyser whether various branches of her organisation have any autonomy, and if so how much.
Hain: Mrs. de Keyser, can you answer that question?
Mrs. de Keyser: Yes, in fact the branches of AAM are entirely autonomous.

Mrs. de Keyser told the jury that AAM's policy was to organise demonstrations outside the grounds of South African matches and coax the big names to come to lead them. At the 1969 annual meeting they had decided to ask the MCC to withdraw its invitation to the South African cricket team, they wrote to cricket teams in the Commonwealth urging them not to participate in any way with the South Africans, and MPs, organisations and charities were contacted. Shortly before the Commonwealth Games in Edinburgh they asked High Commissioners in London if they would reconsider their country's participation in the Games if the South Africans came to Britain to play cricket. Hain was only a few minutes extracting what evidence he wanted from his witness, but Mrs. de Keyser's cross-examination lasted for several hours. In all Stable asked her 218 questions, but he never ruffled her composure nor did she say anything which the prosecutor was later able to make use of in his final address to the jury.

She said that AAM organised the demonstration outside South Africa House to greet the rugby players, which was part of the particulars of offence against Hain. It was AAM's practice for such a demonstration to inform as many people as possible, and Hain and STST would have been contacted. AAM had a representative, Alan Brooks, at the inaugural meeting of STST, as did many other organisations. Stable then turned to AAM's annual meeting of 1969. It became apparent to your observer listening to the scores of questions he fired at Mrs. de Keyser that the prosecution was working from a transcript of a tape recording secretly made at the meeting. Mrs. de Keyser said they had not taken a full report of the meeting, merely noted the resolutions and records of the voting.

The meeting was at the National Liberal Club, its normal venue. Stable said it was attended by 74 people but the witness estimated it was double that. The press were not admitted but there were journalists present who were members. Stable rattled off a list of names of people he said had been elected to the national committee and asked if it was correct. "I really would not be able to say on oath who were members of the national committee at that time", replied Mrs. de Keyser. "I cannot remember accurately." Stable rapped out: "Be kind enough to check up overnight", and continued to read out more names. He asked about the business of the meeting and the witness said it was so far past, with other meetings intervening, that she could not be sure of the details. The judge pressed her: "Please check any records or documents to enable you to answer these questions", but how she was going to conjure them into the witness box at that time remained a mystery to your observer. A very confident Stable continued:

Stable: Would I be right in thinking that you first of all discussed the question of British capital investments in South Africa and Rhodesia? Let me know if I can refresh your memory further (he gave a list of speaker's names).
Mrs. de Keyser: I cannot recollect specifically in this instance of the speaking. This is certainly a subject that would be discussed at our AGM. But I cannot recollect in any details.

She agreed that the meeting passed a resolution calling for a campaign against the General Electric Company which included the words "by direct action if necessary". By this they meant attending company meetings, raising the question of wage rates and so forth. The discussion at the meeting then turned to the rugby tour.

Stable: I suggest that the first person to speak on this subject was Mr. Paul Hodges and that he spoke on the formation of Stop the Seventy Tour. "Detailed plans had already been made to harass the Springbok rugby tour that was due to start at Oxford on November 5." Do you recall this?
Mrs. de Keyser: No, I do not.
Stable: Do you recall him speaking at all?
Mrs. de Keyser: Vaguely, yes.
Stable: Do you recall him saying that he appreciated that the Anti-Apartheid Movement could not be linked officially with the protests?
Mrs. de Keyser: No, I do not.
Stable: Do you recall him saying at the meeting that the Anti-Apartheid Movement's association with the Stop the Seventy Tour campaign had got to be somewhat circuitous because of the methods that were to be employed by STST?
Mrs. de Keyser: No, I do not recall that.
Stable: Just let's go on then.
Mrs. de Keyser: I am just a little surprised, because as the AGM of the Anti-Apartheid Movement is open to all its members and as there are no records of this meeting, I am surprised that there could have been some record taken to use to question me as a witness.

Stable: That is not for you to ask, madam. I am not going to tell you. The respectable front of the Anti-Apartheid Movement which you are employed full time to present to the world is not quite the same pretty face when the press are excluded and no records are going to be kept.

Hain: Objection. I do not see where this is getting us.

Mrs. de Keyser: My Lordship, the membership of the Anti-Apartheid Movement includes people from all walks of life, everyone is welcome at the AGM, and no records are taken because it is a cumbersome task.

Judge: Apart from the records of the resolutions passed, does no one make a note of the persons present?

Mrs. de Keyser: No, but all membership is checked. There is no register taken. Last year we did tape record the whole day, but we have no use for this recording. It is a very lengthy procedure.

Judge: Yes, but it would have been some use to you now.

Mrs. de Keyser: Perhaps, yes, but we have records of the resolutions, that covers a lot of ground.

Judge: Yes, but now you have no record of what was said.

Mrs. de Keyser: Well yes, that is true.

Stable: You know better than anyone probably what limits people can go to in protesting and at what point they break the law. You must have applied your mind to this in the past, being a professional organiser. We have already established your official front was that nothing unlawful was going to be done by AAM as such.

Mrs. de Keyser: Everything we do is perfectly open and public.

Stable: If you join, yes. But the public is not admitted, the press are not admitted and you have no records.

Mrs. de Keyser: I do not put the same implications on this as you do. What you have said is incorrect.

Stable: All that is a perfectly legal activity.

Mrs. de Keyser: Anyone is welcome to join the Anti-Apartheid Movement, there is only a small fee; one is informed about all the activities that are planned.

Judge: The Anti-Apartheid Movement acts wholly within the law, but on this occasion there was a discussion of matters other than within the law.

Mrs. de Keyser: I do not honestly recollect that discussion.

Stable: Let me jog your memory. Do you remember Mr. Paul Hodges saying that he would welcome this, the protests, the serving of a prison sentence for a sit-down strike or some other peaceful form of protest he would accept? Do you remember that? Do you remember Mr. Hain emphasising that the officers of AAM were aware of the plans that he and his front were organising? Do you recall him saying that?

Mrs. de Keyser: I do not actually remember.

Hain: With respect, my witness has already said that she can remember very little, I do not see how she can remember some of this.

Stable: Can you tell the jury why your memory was much better when I was talking about British capital investments, you remember that well, and the resolution, as opposed to your sketchy recollection about STST?

Mrs. de Keyser: The information you mentioned about GEC is a fact and so I remembered that because it was likely to come up at that time, but the details and specific issues of STST escape me.

Judge: Have you any recollection of Mr. Hain's contribution at this meeting?

Mrs. de Keyser: It was three years ago now, I cannot recollect.

Stable: Do you remember a question coming from the floor of the meeting whilst he was speaking and Mr. Ennals, chairman of the meeting, interrupting and stating that as they were aware of the activities planned to stop the rugby tour it was important that no publicity should be given to it by any of the members following the meeting.

Mrs. de Keyser: I do not remember that actually being said. I remember it being reported to have been said.

Stable: Mr. John Ennals said that the officers of AAM were aware of what was being planned by Mr. Hain and his friends to stop the rugby tour and it was important that no publicity on STST should leak to the press.

Mrs. de Keyser: I find that a little strong. I think that in fact there was one press man there, who was a member of the movement.

Stable: Is it right that for many years prior to 1969 there had been a report of the Anti-Apartheid Movement published in a paper that was called *The Morning Star?*

Mrs. de Keyser: I would not know that because in fact it was not recorded. What happens is that after the meeting, if there is a particular resolution, we give it out to all the newspapers.

Stable: And I want to go further with you about this. In fact not a single thing got into the press about what had transpired at this meeting?

Mrs. de Keyser: You would know better than I on this point. I think our only report was written up at that time and we put it out together with a statement of the AGM.

Judge: Did you keep cuttings?

Mrs. de Keyser: We have a cuttings file, yes.

Stable: I suggest that there was on the agenda for the meeting a resolution in relation to the Stop the Seventy Tour and one of the sponsors that morning was Mr. Alan Brooks. Mr. Alan Brooks is AAM's full-time organiser.

Mrs. de Keyser: In 1969.

Stable: I suggest that before the meeting his name was crossed off the agenda so that he did not appear as a sponsor of the resolutions that were ultimately passed.

Mrs. de Keyser: It might be useful to try and let me find the resolutions passed at this meeting.

Stable: That is not necessary, Mrs. de Keyser, because I am able to refresh your memory.

Judge: For the moment you must just answer to the best of your ability.

Stable: It is an unusual situation that when your full-time organiser was down on the agenda as one of the sponsors of the resolution to put it forward at the meeting in respect of STST that his name should be erased so that he should not be present.

Mrs. de Keyser: Perhaps he changed his mind.

Stable: Possibly, but he is not a man who changes his mind, is he?

Mrs. de Keyser: I am not qualified to say that, he has the right to change his mind.

Stable: The reason why he was taken off the motion was because the motions were really not in keeping with the lawful respectable image of AAM which you are employed to uphold.

Mrs. de Keyser: I object to that, my Lordship. I am not employed to uphold any image, I am not employed to pretend anything. It was because he no longer wanted his name to be there.

Stable: Was there another speaker, the second speaker, a man called Peter Hellyer?

Mrs. de Keyser: I know Peter Hellyer is on the executive committee.

Stable: Did he say particularly that they wanted young people to assist them in the public disorder planned for the next few weeks? Do you remember him saying this?

Mrs. de Keyser: I do not remember his speaking at all.

Stable: Was the next speaker Ruth Bundy?

Mrs. de Keyser: No, I do not know, I am not always present all the time.

Stable: Cast your mind back and tell me who the fourth speaker was.

Mrs. de Keyser: On this resolution? I do not know — are you suggesting it was me?

Stable: Yes I am. You know a lot more than you are letting on.

Mrs. de Keyser: This has taken place three years ago. We have since had masses of meetings, I have a diminished memory so far as I am concerned. I will have to go over the records.

After offering the names of other speakers, Stable returned to the subject of direct action.

Stable: Is your memory good enough to tell me whether the words "direct action" featured in the first of these two resolutions?

Mrs. de Keyser: Certainly, the words direct action would have been used on that occasion.

Stable: In the course of your association with Mr. Hain and STST did you come to know what he meant by direct action?

Mrs. de Keyser: I thought what he meant was much the same as we meant.

Stable: Getting inside the grounds where the games were being played with the object of disrupting? What is your understanding of what Mr. Hain meant by direct action?

Mrs. de Keyser: This is not a term that I use or that is particularly meaningful —

Stable: It does not need a speech from you.

Mrs. de Keyser: Don't cut me off when I am speaking. If you stand in a demonstration, you can have violence but you confront the members of the team. That is direct action, that is what we meant. So far as I know, Peter Hain was doing much the same.

Stable: He defines it in his book. Have you read it, incidentally?

Mrs. de Keyser: I have read bits of it.

Stable: Did you understand that direct action meant the actual disruption of matches rather than the more traditional picketing outside the grounds?

Mrs. de Keyser: Not specifically, no.

Stable: And you say the whole of direct action is really judged as to how effectively it disrupts a match and how long? What I am going to suggest to you is this, that throughout the STST campaign, as an organisation AAM was careful only to show itself as organising demonstrations outside the grounds which are perfectly lawful things for movements to take part in. Did you know before that meeting what the STST plans were, and that those plans were to get inside the grounds and stop play?

You knew that?

Mrs. de Keyser: No, I certainly did not.

Stable: What do you think those resolutions meant?

Mrs. de Keyser: The resolutions meant different things. You can choose to interpret them differently. At the AGM there was no question of anyone embarking on protest activities that were unlawful. Under the law, we believed in protests. We do not ourselves organise this kind of protest.

Stable took de Keyser step by step through all the marches against the rugby tour, trying to show the link with Hain, and probing to see if AAM was involved. She emphasised that AAM members were free to act as they pleased and they had no control over them. Stable pressed on to the practice by two young men of how to lock themselves to goalposts before being arrested by police.

Stable: I take it that you didn't join in the hilarious few hours in the garden behind Mr. Hain's house watching these matters rehearsed?

Mrs. de Keyser: I have never been to Mr. Hain's house.

Stable: May I take it that your organisation didn't plan the waylaying of the coach that was to take the South Africans to the ground?

Mrs. de Keyser: No, we did not.

Next day Hain briefly re-examined Mrs. de Keyser after the marathon cross-examination. His main question was as follows:

Hain: Stable seemed better informed than you about the annual meeting of 1969. To your knowledge have South African police spies been at AAM meetings?

Mrs. de Keyser: Yes, we think this has happened.

Hain: Were your headquarters broken into by them?

Mrs. de Keyser: It was broken into. We never established who had broken in. Nobody was caught for doing so.

CHAPTER XV

A Chaotic End—or Tactics?

John Pardoe, Liberal MP for North Cornwall, told the jury that he had known Hain politically and socially for three years. From the manner of Hain's questions it seemed that big things were to be expected from Pardoe but they did not materialise.

Hain: Did you advocate at the 1969 Liberal Party conference that people should go onto the pitch to interrupt play?
Pardoe: Yes. I think it was a short phrase in a long speech off the cuff and among other things that protesters might consider going onto the pitch. It was one of these things.
Hain: Was that statement made in agreement with me?
Pardoe: I am not aware of having made any agreement with you?

Stable apparently noted the hedging in answering the question and picked up this point immediately he began cross-examination seconds later.

Stable: Are you telling the jury that you have publicly advocated that people should object to South Africans playing cricket in this country by going onto the pitch during play?
Pardoe: Provided that they did so in protesting peacefully, yes, but I must make it clear that that was a short phrase in a long speech.
Stable: You must be a responsible person as an MP and must be considered as such.
Pardoe: I can't deny it.
Stable: You advocated people going onto pitches to stop play?
Pardoe: Yes.
Stable: With what object did they go onto pitches?
Pardoe: To bring to the attention of the government and the MCC the strong feeling that there was against playing against the team.
Stable: There are many ways of doing that? You could ask questions in the House?
Pardoe: Yes, as a Member of Parliament one recognises that governments are subject to all sorts of pressures and what isolates an issue is not just parliamentary questions. There are as well the effects of protests outside.
Stable: There are many ways of protesting lawfully, are there not?
Pardoe: Yes.
Stable: You can hold assemblies lawfully?
Pardoe: Yes.
Stable: You can march lawfully?
Pardoe: Yes.
Stable: You know perfectly well that you can organise marches with the advice,

approval and help of the police in this country.

Pardoe: Yes.

Stable: The press and the media generally are open to minority groups?

Pardoe: To a certain extent, yes.

Stable: You recognise, do you not, that there are certain limits to what you may do lawfully?

Pardoe: Yes.

Stable: Would you agree that those limits are the limits which are delineated by the law of the land?

Pardoe: Yes.

Stable: Do you consider it inconsistent with your position to publicly advocate the breaking of the law?

Pardoe: No.

Stable: You don't consider it?

Pardoe: No.

Stable: When you advocated that people should go onto pitches, did you intend that they should go onto pitches in numbers?

Pardoe: No, it was in answer to a question and it was in particular to the questioner who asked it.

Stable: I thought it was a small phrase in a long speech?

Pardoe: The meeting was one at which I was making a speech. Someone interposed a question.

Stable: Could you tell me what the interjection was?

Pardoe: I think somebody shouted, "What action should we take?".

Stable: What was your answer?

Pardoe: Well, it was reported in the press in various different forms. I reeled off a series of things which people could do, and I understand that one of the things I mentioned was, "of course if you want to, go onto pitches". It was something of that short. I can't recall the exact words.

Judge: For what purpose?

Pardoe: As a protest. I thought I had made it clear that I never advocated that people should go on while play was in progress.

Stable: Did you tell them as a public figure, while advocating methods by which the tour could be influenced, that of course you were only referring to the interval or the lunch break?

Pardoe: No, of course I didn't.

Stable: You were advocating the invasion of pitches if games took place?

Pardoe: I am not saying that. I am not agreeing with your word invasion, Mr. Stable, it is a highly emotive phrase.

Stable: Could you turn to page 200? What Mr. Hain describes as STST's direct action tactics: "Invasions of the field". Do you advocate that as a method of protest?

Pardoe: I never have done and I wouldn't know —

Stable: Disruptions, which means disruptions by physical means, of play whilst in progress. Would you advocate that?

Pardoe: No, I would not.

Stable: Sit downs on the field of play during play? Would you advocate that?

Pardoe: I would advocate sit downs but not sit downs during play. But it doesn't mean that to a reasonable man.

Stable: It does in the context of this paragraph, I can assure you.

Judge: Are you meaning a sit down of spectators on an empty pitch?

Pardoe: There is a long period beforehand.

Judge: On the same day?

Pardoe: There would not be much point any other day.

Stable: There is not much point in sitting on the pitch if at the point when the clock gets to the time for the match to start all the protesters get up and leave.

Pardoe: Tremendous point. To ensure that the cheers for the cricket players were not the only sound that was heard by South African ears in this country and it would emphasise —

Stable: That you advocated it, but not while play was taking place?

Pardoe: No.

Stable: Would you agree that it would be wrong to advocate it and to do it during play?

Pardoe: I think it would be wrong of someone in my position to advocate it. It is not for me to make judgements about other people's conscience.

Stable: Obstruction of coach journeys by sitting down in front of the bus that the players were going to use?

Pardoe: In certain circumstances, sitting down in the public highway would be a perfectly legitimate form of protest, yes, provided it is done peacefully.

Stable: Perfectly legitimate? Is that really your considered view of what is lawful?

Judge: You say you had one term in law school. I think you needed a little more.

Pardoe: Yes.

Judge: I suggest you look at the matter again.

Pardoe: I have searched the laws of Parliament and I understand that you have given a ruling in this court that certain matters of the law of trespass are other than as I understand them. I recognise the common law but I should be most grateful for a little guidance.

Judge: If you find time to attend the end of the trial you will hear the guidance I give to the jury on this matter. I can't do more.

Stable: When you advocated in a small phrase the going onto pitches if you want to, did you think you were going to be understood as going onto pitches otherwise than during play?

Pardoe: I certainly would not have thought that the phrase which I would have indicated anything that you could call disruption. I wrote a letter to the *Times* at the time explaining what I had said and what I had meant. It was not published. It made it quite clear in the letter.

This was the last day of the trial so far as witnesses were concerned. There were so many objections by the prosecution — supported by the judge — to the nature of Hain's questions to his witnesses that their periods in the witness box were of a short duration. Hain began firing questions at witnesses hoping they would answer before an objection could be lodged and sometimes succeeded. For instance, former Labour MP Peter Jackson earned a judge's rebuke for answering the following question after the judge had warned him to wait for a ruling as to admissability.

Hain: Is it right, Mr. Jackson, that you have publicly said you would run on a pitch during the cricket tour?

Jackson: I did say that.

Judge: I told you not to answer but you didn't wait.

The Bishop-in-exile of Damaraland, South Africa, Colin Winter, received such a battery of objections to his evidence which was to have been about reactions in South Africa to the rugby and cricket demonstrations, that his appearance was virtually pointless and he walked out of court looking hurt and angry. The *Times* 'Diary' had reported that Anthony Wedgwood Benn, then chairman of the Labour Party, and David Steel, the Liberal chief whip, would be giving evidence at the trial. The prosecution must have seen this news item and intended to object, on perfectly correct legal grounds, that such witnesses had no part to play in the trial. Bishop Winter appeared to have been made the example.

This may have been counter-productive because the jury — composed of course of laymen and not lawyers — might have thought that evidence was being stifled. The arguments about admissability of evidence which they heard were so tortuous and obscure that they were unlikely to have understood them fully. So the evidence of the trial ended suddenly on the dramatic note of the last witness walking out in a huff, and Hain protesting that legal etiquette was preventing him from making a full defence. Certainly, from the verdict which the jury finally returned, it seemed that the confusion quite likely affected them.

Stable was put in the position of having to open his final speech for the prosecution at 3.30 pm on a Thursday, then talking all through Friday. This is a situation most lawyers dread because the jury tend to forget the arguments over the weekend and come fresh on Monday to hear the defence's final speech. Yet Stable is too experienced a lawyer to let that handicap show when he rose to speak.

CHAPTER XVI

"Nothing to do with Apartheid"

In his final speech Stable was soon to the basic reason for having the trial:

"I told you when I opened the case that I hoped the case would highlight the limits to which protests might go in the way of mass demonstration without committing any criminal offence. I also said that the judge's charge to you on the law might well turn out to be an historical charge of great means. At this stage I would like to sound a word of warning. You have not heard a word from me from start to finish attacking Mr. Hain's sincerity. Nor have you heard a word from me supporting South Africa's treatment of its coloured population. The fact is that Mr. Hain is sincere about a matter which a large number of people in England feel as he does.

"I would beg you not to bring in a verdict which is determined by your own views on apartheid, on Mr. Hain's sincerity, on the moderate, intelligent manner in which he has conducted himself in this court. If you allowed this to sway you it would muddle the situation instead of clarifying it. It is well to remember that the law has to be of universal application. If your verdict was one of guilty it would not mean simply that Mr. Hain would not repeat what he did, it would mean that no-one may behave in the way he did, without committing an offence.

"If your verdict was one of not guilty it would not only be an encouragement to him to repeat the same burning issue of apartheid, what he did might be taken as an encouragement to others to adopt Mr. Hain's methods.

"If in your verdict you say Mr. Hain did no more than what he had his rights to do, just consider what that would lead to. If Mr. Hain may behave like he did, why may not persons in the Jewish fraternity band together and break up performances of the Russian ballet by invading the stage and sitting on it next time the Russian ballet comes to London, because there are many who are appalled at the signs of anti-semitism in Russia today? If Mr. Hain may behave like he did why should not an Arab community in England band together and mess up performances by the many Israeli artists. I have taken two examples and thus the state of the world is such today you can probably think up for yourselves dozens of other examples . . .

"My Lord mentioned in the course of the trial what he thought as the social feeling of the homeless. Many people deeply concerned with that issue have joined together into societies to try to do something about it. If Mr. Hain has a right to do what he did they, in my submission, would have a right also to take the law into their own hands and organise the planning of squatters into every new house or every new flat as it is completed. Just suppose you had had a long frustrating wait on the housing list for a new council house, or just suppose you had had a long hard struggle to save a deposit on a house and find a building society to lend you the rest of the price, and just suppose you have been alloted a long-awaited council house, or have found the house you want to buy and have saved up the deposit to buy, and you are making your arrangement at this time to move in on September 1st, you have put off your annual holiday till then and you are going to move to your accommodation.

"How would you feel if, say, Shelter, a completely worthy organisation who had done much to relieve the sufferings of the homeless, had organised that every time a council house became empty and every time a new house was completed by the builders and available for selling, that a homeless family was to be put in possession of it simply by squatting there. Just imagine your own feelings if you arrived at a house which had either been alloted to you by the council or you had saved up to buy only to find that an organised body had arranged to take it over and squat there. Would you be satisfied to know that you could bring a law suit against the squatting family in the civil court and obtain after weeks of delay an order for possession from the civil court, and having got an order against family A when you eventually tried once more to take possession of what was yours to possess, you found these organisers had switched family A out of it and put family B in, and your court order which named family A was not valid so that you had to start proceedings all over again. And it follows that having taken proceedings against family B and there is no reason why the same organisers could not switch family B for family C and keep you out almost indefinitely.

"Actually something very like that was attempted in 1946 just after the war, by a a political organisation, organised by a Mr. Bramley and some of his friends. The reason it has not been repeated is that a jury said by its verdict that Mr. Bramley and his friends who had organised the thing were acting unlawfully and were guilty of conspiracy. Mr. Bramley and his friends, having been convicted by a court of law, which prevented them and everyone else from trying it on again. In that case no-one questioned Mr. Bramley's sincerity, he wanted to help the homeless, but his sincerity was not relevant to the jury's verdict, but that is not a matter for you or for me. Whilst Mr. Sherrard (defence counsel until dismissed by Hain) and I were arguing about the law I read the learned judge the summing up which the judge in that case had given to the jury and it was my submission that the legal facts which applied in the Bramley case are identical to the principles which apply to this case. You will see when the judge in this case comes to direct you as to the legal principles to be applied how far he considered that case to be governed by the same legal principles as this one.

"The point of straying from South African cricket, tennis and rugby matches to performances by the Russian ballet to concerts by Israeli artists and to squatters being put into other people's houses is because the legal principles in my submission is the same and it is not really to the particulars of the case in which it was laid down.

"Mr. Hain plans more direct action demonstrations. If you look at his book, chapter 18, which starts on page 224, we get a chapter entitled "The future campaign" We have evidence that Mr. Hain was convicted of a criminal offence at Bow Street Magistrates Court in 1971 arising out of an incident during a demonstration in June of 1971.

"In his speech to you he said 'I am not a law breaker, I have never equated my beliefs with law breaking'. I am a little sceptical to the accuracy of that temperate speech. But giving as much weight as is possible to what he said, it would at least seem as if he would like to know how far he can go in his future campaigns. It would be much better for him to be told so by you before he sets about increasing un-employment in this country and unemployment amongst the coloured population in South Africa by using direct action against those companies who buy South African goods for distribution in England.

"I want to confine the rest of what I say to a few comments on the so-called defence which Mr. Hain has put forward. His opening speech sounded very moderate and temperate, but if you look at what he said in the light of evidence that is before you you will discover first that, even if this is entirely accurate, it does not constitute a defence, and second, it cannot all be true because it completely contradicts what he has written in his book. He said in opening to you 'I only played a small part, I was the public spokesman not the organiser'. Members of the jury, first of all, if there was a conspiracy as, I submit, there clearly was, to hinder and disrupt the rugby tour and a conspiracy to prevent the cricket tour by becoming the public spokesman he joins the conspiracy and it would have been sufficient had I been able to prove to your satisfaction no more than that he was the public spokesman."

CHAPTER XVII

"Scapegoat Prosecution"

The following Monday morning Peter Hain began a speech which was to last two days, no mean achievement for a 20-year old student. Not that it was a great speech, nor particularly eloquent; he simply set out to hammer home to the jury the rightness of his cause, using repetition of points and numerous analogies to make his arguments. No lawyer would have been permitted to constantly return to the same theme in one speech, but such is the tradition of scrupulous fairness of the British courts to a man defending himself that Hain was permitted considerable latitude.

Hain was faced with the prospect of a jail sentence unless he could firstly convince the jury of the need to have acted in the way he did against the Springbok rugby tour and the white South African cricket tour and, secondly, show that the law of conspiracy should not be extended to embrace his type of political activities.

"A famous writer once described a jury as the twelve persons chosen to decide who has the better lawyer," began Hain. "I am sorry, in a way, that I deprived you of this task because I am not a lawyer and after this experience have no desire of ever becoming one. At times I have felt like a chess novice, watched by a selected audience and the world press as he plays a game against two grand masters simultaneously. The reason I decided to defend myself was not taken lightly but because I wanted to explain to you the reality of the case as I saw it, and I remind you that the phrase 'reality of the case' was the prosecution's and not mine. I don't have anything to hide and I don't have anything to regret about my activity in relation to the Stop the Seventy Tour campaign. I stress *my activities* because there were a number of events, a number of aspects to the campaign, which I would be as unhappy about as no doubt you would be. We are here concerned about my role.

"Because I defended myself you may be encouraged to think that it was wrong of me to call some of the witnesses which I did. I think it is important that you know that this case has been prepared for several months now by Mr. Sherrard and Mr. Capstick and those witnesses I called and many more besides were judged to have important things to say to disprove my guilt.

"The point of saying this at this stage is that I wish to make it clear that I didn't intend to turn this trial into a public meeting, but, I think, equally we may well have reached a stage of a public meeting when Mr. Stable began his final speech. Members of the jury, did it sound to you like a dispassionate Crown prosecutor addressing his mind fairly to the issues in question? Did it? I think I should also say since although I am a British subject I spent most of my life in South Africa that I am very glad I am facing these charges in Britain and not South Africa where the Government has done away with juries . . .

"You see that Exhibit One of the trial is my book and the prosecution have presented it to you as some latter-day 'Mein Kampf' — an interpretation which never occurred to book reviewers when it was published.

"Let me remind you that it was some two and a half years ago that this prosecution was born on 22 May 1970, when Mr. Bennion publicly announced his intention to prosecute me. That was the day of the cancellation of the cricket tour. Since then we have had a number of ups and downs. To cut a long story short, when my book was published on 21 January 1971 a further stage in the prosecution developed and firm measures were taken to lay summonses. The point I wish to make is that it has been a prosecution which has been over my head for a very long time. It is a prosecution brought not by the Director of Public Prosecutions but by a private citizen. You will see that on the back of your copy of the indictment it is now no longer even a private citizen but a private citizen, Mr. Bennion, on behalf of a limited company, Freedom Under Law Limited. I think these points are important by way of stating the context of my submissions on the evidence. You have heard as well of the nature of the prosecution. From Wilf Isaacs, a prosecution witness, of fund-raising tours in South Africa to collect money to support this prosecution. You have heard of a collection which ran in South Africa for some time over that period with the 'Pain for Hain' slogan. You have heard from another witness, Mr. Wates, for the defence, that white South Africans regarded this trial as a means of making me a scapegoat. You have heard, too, of other fund raising expeditions in relation to this prosecution. This is a South African-inspired prosecution and I believe you need to bear this in mind."

After meticulously disecting the evidence against him and seeking to demonstrate that if the jury looked at another part of his book they would find evidence which explained his actions, or showed that they were really the actions of others which he was merely recounting as an author, Hain then turned to the subject of non-violent direct action. This was his view of it:

"Non-violent direct action in all circumstances does not involve physical violence of any sort and always falls short of intentional damage. Above all, direct action is essentially lawful only in circumstances where it may be alleged to be unlawful — that is in those murky and vague areas of the law. For example, conspiracy to trespass where, everybody, if I may say so, including judges, in past cases are confused. Direct action is essentially a personal form of action springing from a personal conscience.

"Conspiracy is in a wholly different category from any of the things I say I did and which have been referred to to try and blur the issue. Mr. Stable said that I had introduced direct action into Britain, but it has in its various forms a long honourable tradition in British society. The law of the land as it now stands contains many provisions as a result of direct action, notably the suffragettes . . .

"I am not charged with climbing over the fence at Twickenham; I am charged with conspiracy to do some 208 particulars and it is that that I dispute very strongly and in my submission the evidence produced does not sustain the indictment. I think it is clear from the submissions I have made to you, and from one of the prosecution witnesses, Mr. Gordon Winter, that the character of those activities was of an information and of a publicity nature, not of a conspiratorial nature . . .

"It was an honest campaign and a book has been written about it by the defendant. It is very difficult to be more public than that. It was in my submission, open and above board, and the charge with which I am indicted, if it were to be sustained, would contradict that basic fact . . .

"As I understand it, the rule of law means the rule that nobody may be imprisoned unless charged and found guilty of an offence against the law of the land. It is therefore fundamental to the rule of law that an individual must know what he may do or may not do within the law of the land, and, members of the jury, you may feel that the law of conspiracy to trespass is unclear."

Here Judge Gillis was quick to interject: "It is not for the jury to decide whether the law is clear or unclear; it is my duty to charge and direct the jury what the law is. Even if they were composed of lawyers of the highest eminence they would not be entitled to go outside what the presiding judge tells them."

Hain then told the jury that the prosecutor, Mr. Stable, had made submissions and statements relating to his integrity and sincerity. "Those submissions were in conflict with each other," said Hain. "I don't intend to defend my sincerity or integrity — it is for you to decide whether they are a relevant part of this case — but I do think that when phrases are used by a Queen's Counsel such as 'Lifting the curtain on Mr. Hain's real character' then it is in fact the point the defence has been making throughout this case is that the indictment must fail because that evidence is not there. Indeed the evidence is so absent that is unnecessary to use that kind of phrase."

Judge: Mr. Hain, you have repeated that phrase six or seven times!

Hain then attacked what he called the "misunderstanding which affects this whole indictment." The prosecution, he said, seriously alleged that he was to be ranked with Mrs. Pankhurst and Ghandi.

"It would be highly flattering if it were not so absurd. They seriously believe and the indictment seriously alleges, that I, Peter Hain, a 19-year old student who lives with his parents and sisters in a house in Putney, galvanised tens of thousands of demonstrators, inspired a whole movement against racist sport, in the same way as Mrs. Pankhurst inspired a whole movement against the oppression of men, and Ghandi inspired a whole movement against racial degradation.

"The people who did the acts alleged in that indictment are legion. They are Maureen Baker in Leeds, Kenneth Chew in Aberdeen, Harry Joshua in Wales.

"I hate apartheid. I have hated it ever since I woke up that morning in Johannesburg to find my parents missing — arrested by the South African Security Police who had come, like thieves in the night, and departed leaving me, a boy of 11, to look after our home and two young sisters. My parents' crime? Belonging to the South African Liberal Party which had blacks as members. Just as you cannot play sport with black people in South Africa, neither can you belong to the same political party. It is against the law. And Mr. Stable says we must always obey laws for no better reason, apparently, than that they are laws. So when the South African sportsmen came, of course I did what I could. I personally entered three sporting arenas — without agreeing with anyone to do so, and leaving without struggling and without being charged with a breach of the law. I debated with people like Wilf Wooler. I became spokesman for STST and for reasons best known to the Press was always quoted in these issues. Conspire, as alleged in this indictment, I did not."

CHAPTER XVIII

"Everyman is under the Law"

Judge Gillis began summing up on the morning of Wednesday, 16 August, and took until Friday afternoon to laboriously retell all the evidence which he considered relevant. It was a long and boring recitation, as are most summings up. One wondered why the witnesses had all been called in the first place to give their testimony — might it not have been quicker for Judge Gillis to have summarised their statements?

By Friday afternoon the Judge had apparently forgotten what he had been saying, for he told the jury: "I availed myself of an opportunity during the (lunch) adjournment which I wished to have of checking my notes and the evidence on two or three matters which I wish to look at again, and I find that I have said what I wish to say about them, so I am sure you will be relieved that there is no need for me to go back to the evidence."

About the politics and morality of the case, Judge Gillis permitted himself these observations:-

"You have heard references to the rights of citizens to protest and demonstrate.

"There have been references to the right of personal freedom to speak out in support of a cause man believes in. That is the right of all men, of all persons in this land. Juries in our history have always been able to protect the undoubted right to protest, the undoubted right to demonstrate which is part of the common law, the heritage of the English way of life. And there is no restriction placed upon the exercise of those undoubted rights save that which comes no doubt from what has been referred to as the rule of law, namely that all men must exercise their rights according to law and within the law. No man has the right with others or by himself to dispense with or suspend, if I may use the language of more modern times, to opt out of a law with which he doesn't agree, which he may find unacceptable as he wishes to deal with his own affairs. We live as you know, members of the jury, in a society governed by law and within the law all men are free to think as they will, speak as they will, to urge their views upon others, lawfully, by lawful means, to seek their support.

"Our society, as you know, is one which is governed by law and a man is entitled to do whatever he thinks right provided always he is not infringing the rights of others or otherwise acting contrary to the law. He may regard another man as lacking in human compassion. He may regard him as a political outcast or merely unworthy. In a free society as this land is he can't dictate to such a man how that man shall think or how that man shall act, or what he shall do or deprive him of the enjoyment of his own rights acting in accordance with his own lawful actions, going about his own affairs in a lawful manner. You will recognise, members of the jury, that the right to protest and the right to demonstrate is a right which has to be exercised within the law and by lawful means and no man if he acts contrary to law can give or provide himself with an answer in law from the fact that he is acting in a way that is morally right and in a manner which he may regard the law as inappropriate or unfair. Those you may realise are some of the basic features of our way of life whereby under the rule of law we secure the rights to all men, the ignorant, the foolish, the indifferent, as well as the wise, the alert and the politically conscious who are morally anxious to serve their fellows. All men in a lawful society must conduct themselves according to law. And, I venture to take time to say, it is because it may well be that in another place on another day you would wish to put yourselves in support of the causes which the defendant manifestly has a part. You are sitting here as judges of the evidence in this trial, not in your private capacity or any personal sense. You have to form your judgement on these charges according to the evidence you have heard. According to the law because if law is betrodden, you may well have to ask yourselves how long will the freedom of any man be secure. When these charges arose, they came as following the arrival in this country of teams of players from South Africa in 1969 and 1970 and following the invitation of a cricket team to tour this country in 1970 and play on the invitation of organisations and men, who had asked those teams to come in 1969/70 to play with their teams on their cricket pitches, on their rugby pitches and also at the tennis tournament in July of 1969.

"There has been a reference more than once necessarily so to what the defendant has described as racialism in sport. You will know from the evidence and indeed from your general knowledge as well, that the government and Parliament of South Africa according to the evidence heard, has for some years adopted a policy with regard to the black and coloured peoples of South Africa known as apartheid. Mr. Hain's book bears the title 'Don't Play With Apartheid'. He explains what he means by that. He defines it, as he is entitled to do, as unworthy racialism, discrimination against men because of their race or colour. You know vast thousands of men seek by various ways to bring pressure to bear on public opinion in South Africa and change its government with the object of putting an end to what they regard as the evil of apartheid. As one witness remarked, not only the well being and interest of those who suffer by it, but because they believe in the end it will bring suffering and harm to all who live in South Africa unless that policy is changed. It is towards the achievement of that object as you know from the evidence, many methods have properly been adopted apart from general propaganda. One method has been to urge or boycott sports teams chosen, as the defendent explains, on principles of apartheid or racialist lines. It was said it is because the visiting teams in 1969 and 70 and the cricket tour planned for 1970 were so chosen that those against apartheid racialism took the steps they did to protest and demonstrate. Lawful protest they were fully entitled to do. Protest against the coming to this country of such teams so chosen, to protest against their being invited here or to play here and that object has not been achieved says the prosecution. The prosecution case is that to achieve that object, the defendant with others combined by unlawful means, that only is the basis of their allegation and it is vital to remember throughout this case that you don't have to make any decisions about policy of apartheid. That's not the issue. You don't have to make any decisions about right to protest against it. That's not an issue, no-one challenges that right. You don't have to make a decision as to what are the best ways to raise opinion against it. Those opinions may differ. All you have to do is to decide the allegations in the indictment. Allegations of conspiracy by making an agreement by unlawful means. The prosecution had submitted that never from the beginning had they or do they urge one word in favour of racialism, it was not part of their case and was outside their submission.

"There has been a reference by the accused that this is a private prosecution. It is. It has always been the right of any man in this country for many centuries to go before a magistrate or justice of the peace and as the phrase is, lay information before that officer, put matters before him and seek the issue of process. The justice of the peace is satisfied that the information permits him to order the issue of a summons or a warrant to issue process requiring the attendance of an accused person and then as I have explained the trial proceeds before the magistrate where the evidence is submitted if the accused has a case to answer, he goes before a jury upon the indictment. Other persons such as the Director of Public Prosecutions and other public authorities including chief constables and chief officers of police have additional rights and duties in regard to the institution of criminal proceedings because of the office they hold but that doesn't deprive the ordinary private citizen of his right to go before a magistrate if he feels he has material proper to submit to the magistrate and seek the issue of indictments. One of the ancient rights whereby the peace of the realm was sustained by the action of a private person. Accordingly, members of the jury, as you examine this case the fact that this is a private prosecution has little if any relevance. At one stage to which I shall in due course come, Mr. Hain said the prosecution against him was oppressive and vindictive and that banners, posters had been seen in South Africa bearing the words 'Pain for Hain'. That this is a South African-inspired prosecution. You may feel that the fact that this is a private prosecution assists you to examine the evidence.

"Mr. Hain said more than once that he didn't deny that the acts referred to in the indictment were in fact committed, did take place, but what he said was denying from the outset was that he took part in any of them by way of a conspiracy and he was submitting from time to time that there was no evidence that he was in conspiracy with anyone in regard to any of those matters. He says as you know that he was taking a part, not a leading part, in helping forward that cause in which he believed and that there was no conspiracy and others were acting independently and spontaneously. He was in combination unlawfully with no-one. And so you will bear those observations in mind, remembering always your overwhelming duty to get a true verdict according to the evidence.

"In the course of the speeches there were references to a number of matters some of which you may think were of no assistance, some of which you may think had the mark of exaggeration or rhetoric upon them. Accordingly, if you think in this that any illustration helped them of course you will benefit by it. If you think it was unhelpful or ill chosen, you will reject it. Obviously there had to be references to South Africa but apart from that you have been taken back to Nazi Germany. References were made to what a man should do if under that foul regime he was required to murder innocent people. You would know that he would not be required to proceed by law in that way. It is extremely important to keep emotion out of your consideration. References to Pankhurst, Ghandi; there were references

122

to Russia, Communism. This is a trial in England with reference to the laws of England. It would be a wise course would it not if you keep your feet on the ground as you examine the evidence."

Soon afterwards Judge Gillis sent the jury home for the weekend with the warning that they would be sent out to consider their verdicts on Monday morning.

CHAPTER XIX

Verdict and Sentence

The last day of the trial was reached on Monday, August 22. It had been a long haul since July 24 when the legal arguments began. In court with Peter, as usual, were his family — Adeline and Walter, his parents, his two sisters and a girlfriend, Verity Burgmann. As ever, Hain was dressed casually but well-turned out. His accuser, Francis Bennion, appeared to have had his hair cut for the occasion and was immaculately dressed in a charcoal suit, mustard shirt with a grey tie. At 10.35 am Judge Gillis packed the jury off to their room for their deliberation. They did not reappear until 4.21 pm when the Judge had to send for them. They told him they were sorry but they had not agreed on a single count against the defendant.

Judge: If there is any matter of law or any part of the evidence with which I can assist you then now is the time to ask.
Foreman of the jury: We have no questions.
Judge: Then I will accept a majority verdict if ten of you are in agreement.

At 5.57 pm the jury trooped back into court and told the Judge that they were agreed by ten votes to two that Hain was guilty of Count 3 (the Davis Cup tennis at Bristol) but they could not agree on counts 1, 2 and 4.

It was evident that Hain had succeeded in going over the heads of the prosecution and the judge and influencing the majority of the jury with his political philosophy. The fact that the jury had no questions to ask of the judge when he recalled them is one pointer to this and is confirmed by the confused verdicts. Hain was obviously delighted and Bennion was impassive. Mark Potter, the junior counsel who had taken over in Stable's absence, asked for a five-minute adjournment. When the court re-assembled Potter made a significant statement:

Potter: Francis Bennion has considered the position. He was looking for a ruling from the court on direct action tactics and that he has obtained. The prosecution was a proper step but it has been a strain for all concerned and we do not wish to impose on anyone the strain of a further trial.
Judge: As there is no application for the indictments to remain on the file, Section 17 of the Criminal Justice Act, 1967, empowers me to direct that verdicts of not guilty be recorded. Or a jury could be sworn in again and another trial commenced. I shall direct that verdicts of not guilty be recorded in counts 1, 2 and 4.
Potter: That would be acceptable.

It now remained for Hain to be sentenced for the one count on which he had been convicted. A detective told the judge that Hain was born in Kenya in 1950, had been educated in Pretoria up to 1966 when he came to England. "He is a student and his home conditions are good", said the policeman.

Hain told the judges he wanted to call two witnesses as to his character and took the opportunity to put in a blow against the conspiracy laws.

"I still am not certain of which particular one I was found guilty", Hain complained.

Judge: You have not been convicted of a particular but a conspiracy.

In his speech to attempt to mitigate the sentence (normally made by the defending counsel) Hain was short and to the point: "It has been agreed during the trial that the tennis indictment is the less important of the four counts. I was not concerned at the time to break any law but to assert the principle of non-racialism in sport. I was the chairman of the Stop the Seventy Cricket Tour and my conscience remains clear."

Lord Avebury, formerly Eric Lubbuck, Liberal MP for Orpington and now a Peer, told the judge that Hain had been elected at 19 a member of the National League of Young Liberals and later became its chairman. "I have found him to be utterly sincere and straightforward and a convinced advocate of non-violence", he added.

The second character witness, Bishop Colin Winter, who was in his diocese, Damaraland, South Africa, during the years of the anti-South African demonstrations, described the impact of the STST campaign. "There was a massive reaction in South Africa because they have things on their conscience," he said.

Once again Judge Gillis began to get uneasy at Bishop Winter's style of evidence. The Judge said no one had challenged Hain's sincerity nor the worthiness of the cause and the impact of the campaign on the South African public was of more concern to a public meeting than to him. Hain pressed his point that he had taken his stand on principle and that the police were fully aware of the actions surrounding the tennis match but he was not charged.

Judge: The jury has found you guilty and it is a serious conviction. You are a young man of undoubted ability and sincerity . . . As high as the great cause is there is a rule of law in this land. If the law is set aside then no man's liberty is safe. I recognise your high moral stand and that you have been convicted in the limited area of Count 3. I recognise your youth and the lack of judgement in your conduct. I will fine you £200 and give you ample time to pay — within three months or three months in prison.

Hain was also ordered to pay £50 towards the costs of his own defence. It is doubtful if the Judge knew at the time that Hain himself would not have to pay the £250 which would be met by the Hain Defence Fund.

From the moment of passing sentence a row began about Bennion's costs which he had stated publicly were around £50,000. Mark Potter, his counsel, told the judge that the Courts Act (Section 47:1) permitted him to apply for costs out of central funds. It was correct, he said, that money had been given for the prosecution by the South African Rugby Board and the Hain Prosecution Fund whose chairman was Ross McWhirter. But, said Potter, after the magistrate issued summonses against Hain, outside fund raising ceased on legal advice and Bennion's own money was used.

Judge Gillis questioned why Wilfred Isaacs and Dawe de Villiers had been brought from South Africa twice whereas once might have been sufficient. (The defence was prepared to have their statements read to the Central Criminal Court.) Isaacs had said in evidence during the trial that he had come to Britain on business but what about de Villiers? Potter replied that it was thought that at least one person should be called "in flesh and blood" to speak about the rugby tour and de Villiers had been the captain. As Potter was pressing for the prosecution's costs to be paid, Hain tried to put his point of view but Potter and the Judge checked him, indicating that it was none of his business.

So the last words of the remarkable trial were said by Judge Gillis: "I propose to adjourn the application for costs. I am much impressed by the number of irrelevancies which have crept into this trial."

Hain and Bennion left the court surrounded by their supporters and held press conferences, each saying they were delighted with the outcome. Significantly, the same day the trial ended there was another event taking place in another part of the world which showed that the issue of racialism in sport was as important as it had been three years previously. All the African nations participating in the 1972 Olympic games at Munich announced that they would walk out if Rhodesia was not expelled. It was the first time the individual African countries had presented a united front on the Rhodesian issue. Between 1969 and 1972 the controversy over racialism in sport had taken on much bigger dimensions as people realised that if they stood firmly together the status quo could be broken.

Two weeks later Judge Gillis announced that Francis Bennion was entitled to his costs out of public funds. "The right of a private person to have unrestricted access to the courts is a centuries-old right . . . that right is a valid weapon in the protection of the ordinary man's own liberties and personal freedoms. It exists until and unless Parliament takes it away. It is not for the court to encourage that erosion."

Several politicians, notably Jeremy Thorpe, the Liberal leader, said publicly that they thought Judge Gillis was wrong, because giving full costs opened the doors to unlimited private prosecutions. Others said that Bennion was entitled to one-fourth of his costs as only one-fourth of the indictment had succeeded. Bennion revealed that he had put some £15,000 of his own money into the case and hoped to recover most of it from the public purse, as the Judge had directed, but two years later Bennion and the taxing office of the Treasury were still arguing over the final figure. And by this time, too, Bennion had resigned as director of Freedom Under the Law Limited — nicknamed "Freedom Under the Lawyer" by its opponents — and was back as a civil servant in his old job as a Parliamentary Counsel drafting government legislation.

Hain's appeal against his conviction was not reached in the Court of Appeal until 22 October 1973 because the case turned on whether conspiracy to trespass is a criminal offence and there was another case running slightly in front of Hain's which was to be the test. In the appendix to this book Geoff Robertson deals with the importance of the Kamara case, as it is known, and all it is necessary to report here is that the House of Lords confirmed that there is such an offence as conspiracy to trespass and Kamara lost his appeal. When Hain's appeal was reached, and argued by Brian Capstick who had assisted in the trial proper, it was little more than a formality. After two hours the Appeal Court judges dismissed the application and Hain was ordered to pay another £150 costs.

All our Conspirators

by Geoff Robertson

Laws are of two different kinds: statute law and common law. Statutes are Acts of Parliament laws passed by elected representatives which have merely to be interpreted and applied by the courts. Common law, on the other hand, is the body of doctrine built up by court decisions over the centuries — 'judge made law' as opposed to laws which originate in the democratic process. Once an Act is passed, it cannot be altered except by another Parliamentary initiative. The common law, however, is constantly being shifted and adapted by judges to meet new situations which are seen as disruptive of civilised society. This process, which undermines the democratic philosophy that all laws must receive the assent of the people's representatives, is sanctioned by the legal tradition that judges only "declare" what the common law has always been, rather than "make" new law. But this is a semantic quibble: their "declaration" of the law necessarily "extends" the common law, with the effect of proscribing conduct which was not previously thought to be criminal: the result is a new law, as surely as if it had been passed by an overwhelming Parliamentary majority.

The doctrine of conspiracy has in recent years proved the most fertile ground for judges and prosecutors to "discover" that old laws meet new situations. "Conspiracy" is an infinitely elastic common law formula which can be stretched to criminalise conduct which Parliament has declined to make specifically illegal. The Hain case provides a classic illustration of common law in the making: it was part of an important legal debate which in the 1970s gave birth to the two common law conspiracies of trespass and intimidation: new and frightening weapons for the authorities to press into service against peaceful protest.

What sort of conduct amounts to a criminal conspiracy? The answer is that it must either be immoral, criminal, or of a kind which could provoke an action for damages in a civil court. The Hain case was not concerned with the "public morals" conspiracies which had been used to silence the "underground press' in the late 1960s. He was charged with conspiracy to commit some minor criminal offences, notably intimidation, punishable by a £20 fine (an illustration of how a trivial offence punishable by a small fine in magistrates' court can be elevated, at least where more than one person is involved, into a crime of the utmost seriousness by using the conspiracy device. Suddenly the penalty is increased from some statutory maximum authorised by Parliament — perhaps a fine, or a short jail sentence — into an offence punishable by life imprisonment).

But the great legal significance of *R v Hain* is in the development of the doctrine that a mere interference with another's legal right may, in certain circumstances, be a serious criminal offence. Civil wrongs, as distinct from crimes, are injuries which the victim himself can remedy by suing for damages.

He has no right to receive police assistance in punishing his opponent. But where two or more persons "conspire" to commit a civil wrong, such as a trespass or a breach of contract, they become subject to the rigors of the criminal law.

In the early 1970s judges decided that agreements to commit civil wrongs and agreements to injure another person in such a way that the "public interest" is involved (e.g. by trespassing on land owned by "the Authorities" or disrupting a sporting event) were indictable as criminal conspiracies. The question of whether the "public interest" is involved was for the judge to decide, and his decision cannot be challenged by the defence or overruled by the jury. *R v Hain* was a case which reaffirmed the power to jail those whose activities conflict with the "public interest" — as divined by judges. The political potential of similar conspiracy decisions in the United States prompted Clarence Darrow to denounce the conspiracy law as "a worn-out piece of tyranny, this dragnet for compassing the imprisonment and death of men whom the ruling class does not like . . .". This rhetoric expresses the same sombre message which heads the chapter on conspiracy in the leading textbook on English Criminal Law:

> "The crime of conspiracy affords support for any who advance the proposition that the criminal law is an instrument of Government"

What is a "conspiracy"? The Oxford Dictionary defines "to conspire" as "to combine privily for an unlawful purpose, especially treason, murder and sedition . . ." But the first lesson juries (and often defendants) learn is that a "conspiracy" in law is merely an agreement, and not necessarily a legally binding or even a serious agreement. "A nod or a wink may amount to a conspiracy" the jury was warned at the Angry Brigade Trial. The "conspiracy" of the Shrewsbury pickets was inferred from the mere fact that they were among 300 workers who invaded certain building sites. When their QC complained that "some of these men met for the first time on these sites" the trial judge interrupted "You know very well it can be a conspiracy when they never met and never knew each other". All the prosecution has to prove at a conspiracy trial is that the defendants made an agreement: if the judge decides that what they have agreed to do is "unlawful", the jury must convict.

"Unlawful" is by no means confined to serious criminal conduct: it includes minor criminal offences, civil wrongs which merely give someone the right to sue for damages (e.g., libel or trespass) and activities which are not against the law at all, but which conflict with the moral values which the judge wishes to uphold. It does not matter that the agreement is never carried out, or even that the conspirator had a change of heart and does all in his power to frustrate its fruition. His guilt is fixed for all time at the very moment that he gives his assent to the plan. Nor does it matter if, at the time they made the agreement, the conspirators did not realise that its object would be declared "unlawful" or "immoral" in future court proceedings. Ignorance of the law is no defence — even when "the law" really means "the prejudices of the judiciary".

The crime of conspiracy entered the law of England in 1304, in the form of an act to punish malicious prosecutions. Edward I's Ordinance of Conspirators defined them as:

"They who do confeder or bind themselves by oath, covenant or other alliance . . . falsely and maliciously to indict or cause to indict, or falsely to move or maintain pleas; and also such as cause children within age to accuse men of felony whereby they are imprisoned and sore grieved".

Several centuries elapsed before the political potential of the conspiracy charge was, in the words of one eminent legal historian, "emphasised by the Star Chamber, which recognised its possibilities as an engine of government and moulded it into a substantive offence of wide scope, whose attractions were such that its principles were gradually adopted by the common law courts . . .". Before its abolition in 1641, the Star Chamber had established that the essence of the crime of conspiracy is the actual agreement, and hence no overt actions need be proved by the prosecution to obtain a conviction. Moreover, conspiracy was no longer limited to actions for malicious prosecution, but extended to agreements to commit all crimes, however trivial. These two cardinal principles are still being applied, by the courts, 300 years later, to situations that Star Chamber judges would never have envisaged. The rule that the crime is committed when the agreement is made was carried to its reductio ad absurdum in 1890, when a woman was convicted of conspiring to procure her own abortion, although she was not in fact pregnant, and although Parliament had expressly excluded an aborted woman from liability when it made abortion a crime in 1861. In 1964 the Court of Appeal reinvigorated the rule that agreements to commit petty offences are punishable by life imprisonment when it approved a charge of conspiracy to contravene the Road Traffic Act, even though the maximum penalty for the actual section which the defendants had agreed to contravene was but a small fine.

The most devastating extension of the conspiracy law since the Star Chamber days was to punish, as though they were serious crimes, agreements to do acts which themselves entailed only civil liability for damages at the complaint of an injured party. The encroachment of this doctrine was stealthy at first, beginning with cases of "conspiracy to defraud" by not paying a civil debt. But in 1832 one judge caught these straws in the wind and wove them into the fabric of the criminal law in a pattern which has had a baleful influence on judicial thinking ever since. Lord Denman defined a conspiracy as "an agreement to do an unlawful act, or a lawful act by unlawful means". "Unlawful" included actions giving rise merely to civil damages.

The immediate casualties of this formula were the incipient Trade Unions, whose every strike or picket was elevated into a criminal conspiracy. A conspiracy conviction exiled the Tolpuddle Martyrs, while "conspiracy to obstruct an employer and interfere with his lawful freedom of action", "conspiracy to annoy and interfere with the masters in the conduct of their business" abound in these nineteenth century industrial cases. In 1871 there is even a case where a group of women were convicted of conspiracy for saying "Bah" to blacklegs. Finally political pressure forced Disraeli to pass the Conspiracy and Protection of Property Act 1875, which abolished conspiracy charges in respect of trade disputes unless they related to agreements to intimidate or to commit crime. This relieved legal pressure on the Trade Unions at the time, but left a loophole which almost a century later was relentlessly exploited by another Tory government to prosecute building workers whose picketing activities, although furthering genuine trade disputes, were alleged to be conspiracies to commit minor criminal offences. The crime of intimidation is defined in Section 7 of the 1875 Act:

"Every person who, with a view to compel any other person to abstain from doing or to do any act which such other person has a legal right to do or abstain from doing, wrongfully and without legal authority

(1) uses violence to or intimidates such other person or his wife, or children, or injures his property; or

(2) persistently follows such other person about from place to place; or . . .

(3) watches or besets the house or other place where such other person resides, or works or carries on business, or happens to be, or the approach to such house or place; or

(4) follows such other person with two or more other persons in a disorderly manner in or through any street or road;

shall on conviction . . . be liable either to pay a penalty not exceeding twenty pounds, or to be imprisoned for a term not exceeding three months".

The language of this section provided an obvious inspiration to the draftsman of the Hain indictment: legal rights to watch and play cricket and football were allegedly infringed by intimidation, persistent following of team members, watching and besetting their hotels, and so on. This device of coupling a conspiracy charge to the minor criminal offence of intimidation was pioneered by Bennion's lawyers. One year later this very same "conspiracy to intimidate" charge was adopted by the Government as a means to put down working class protest of the "flying picket" variety which had erupted during the building workers' strike. The Home Secretary urged police to prosecute for intimidation, especially since "The law as it stands . . . makes it clear that sheer numbers attending can of itself constitute intimidation". His first victims were convicted and imprisoned at Shrewsbury for conspiring to contravene the very Act which had been designed, in 1875, to end conspiracy prosecutions of Trade Unionists.

The Hain case also made its contribution to the startling legal discovery that an agreement to commit a trespass — a mere temporary presence on another's property without permission — constitutes a serious criminal offence if the public interest is deemed (by the judge) to be at stake. We have seen that it was theoretically always possible to charge with conspiracy those who agree to do actions which would give others a right to sue for damages. But since the 1875 legislation, the "unlawful act" charged was always in prosecuting practice either criminal, immoral, or at least accompanied by fraud or malice. Mere trespass did not qualify as an "unlawful act" until 1946, when one Bramley was convicted at the Old Bailey for his part in housing homeless ex-Servicemen in disused Army shelters. His trial judge, Sir Hugh Stable, ruled that an agreement to trespass was a criminal offence whenever the public interest was involved. But the Bramley case was never fully reported and its implications were forgotten, so that by 1969 a leading textbook on criminal law could confidently state "an agreement to commit a civil trespass is not indictable". One man who had understandably not forgotten the Bramley ruling, however, was the judge who made it. In February, 1969, during the furore over "direct action" against Springbok tours Sir Hugh wrote to the

Daily Telegraph, urging that Peter Hain be prosecuted for criminal conspiracy to trespass — modestly omitting to mention that the main authority for the existence of such a law was his goodself. Francis Bennion duly complied, acknowledging his debt, perhaps, by briefing Sir Hugh's son, Mr. Owen Stable, QC, to bring Hain to justice.

The political potential of the Stable family heirloom was no longer lost on the prosecuting authorities: they took advantage of it in 1971 to convict some Sierra Leone students who had occupied their country's High Commission, acting, as Lord Hailsham conceded, "from a genuine sense of grievance" against a government they believed "arbitrary, tyrannical and unconstitutional". Obviously it had become time to decide whether "conspiracy to trespass" really did exist in criminal law and these students were made the reluctant guinea pigs. From a civil liberties viewpoint they set an unfortunate example, because their occupation involved an unacceptable degree of force — threats with toy guns which the victims believed were real and imprisonment of High Commission staff. Hain, whose direct action tactics were determinedly non-violent, had his appeal against conviction shelved until the House of Lords could decree what the law really was. The efforts of the students' counsel, Sir Dingle Foot, to confine the scope of the conspiracy laws were unavailing.

Lord Hailsham approved conspiracy prosecutions of the parties to agreements which would, if carried out, give an aggrieved individual the right to sue for more than nominal damages, e.g., for breach of contract, trespass or libel, *or* where execution of the agreement 'invades the domain of the public', e.g., by trespassing on land owned by the Government or by disrupting a sporting event. The Sierra Leone Embassy decision, delivered in June 1973, will have a chilling effect on political protest. Already nine Welsh language protestors have been tried at the Old Bailey for conspiring to trespass in a BBC studio, although they had never acutally set foot on BBC property. In Birmingham five building workers were charged with conspiracy to trespass when they entered the offices of a local firm to protest, at the instigation of their trade union, against the firm's practice of supplying "lump labour" to builders. Three television cameramen who followed to film their arrest were charged with the same offence: a sinister example of how the new crime can be used to inhibit the press.

A few months later, Hain's appeal came before the Court of Appeal, which seized the opportunity to throw the conspiracy net even wider. Hain, it will be remembered, was convicted of a conspiracy to interfere with the lawful rights of persons to watch a David Cup match against South Africa by running onto the Court and distributing anti-apartheid leaflets. His trial judge instructed the jury that they should find him guilty if he interfered with the public's rights by unlawful methods which are "of substantial public concern — something of importance to citizens who are interested in the maintenance of law and order". This means that demonstrators commit a crime punishable by life imprisonment if they interfere with public "rights" (whatever they are) by methods which agitate the "law and order" brigade, although the methods themselves are not illegal.

At the appeal, Hain's counsel argued that a handful of Young Liberals running across a tennis court, causing no damage, using no force and disrupting play only for a very short time, were not employing "unlawful means of substantial public concern". Lord Justice Roskill riposted "Hain would not have done it had it not been a matter of public concern". The court incorporated this circular argument into its judgement: "the whole object of the exercise would not be achieved if the event had not aroused widespread public interest". In other words, effective protest *by definition* involves matters of "substantial public concern" because the court equates this with "attracting public attention" which it uncharitably assumes to be the purpose of all protest demonstrations. On this interpretation, even token interruptions of events — John Arden leaping onto the Aldwych stage to confront the Royal Shakespeare company's performance of his play "The Island of the Mighty", pram-pushing mothers stopping traffic to demand a pedestrian crossing; hecklers drowning out a politician at a public meeting — are now all within the dragnet of criminal conspiracy. At the end of the day, we have the spectre of an infinitely elastic formula, devised by the Star Chamber and gratefully adopted by modern judges and prosecutors as an instrument for convicting those who would otherwise not be indicted at all because no existing crime outlawed their conduct. Legal ingenuity for its own sake is counterproductive when it fashions new laws without reference to the democratic process, and when it opens up a wide field of uncertainty as to what conduct is in fact criminal. It is to the fundamental precepts of the criminal law, and the threat to them posed by conspiracy, that we must now turn.

Dicey, the great constitutional theorist, considered that the chief requirement of "The Rule of Law" was certainty: no citizen should be declared a criminal unless he had broken a specific rule established before he offended against it. Ignorance of the law is no defence — *provided* the law is both comprehensible and accessible to all citizens. Jeremy Bentham further demanded that criminal laws should carry a recognisable tariff of punishments, so that their deterrent effect can operate at the point when a potential criminal is weighing his risks. He is hardly likely to be deterred if he is unaware that his contemplated action is in fact criminal, or if he has no conception of the severity of the sentence it will merit. Thus certainly is the very cornerstone of the criminal law, cherished in England as a guarantee of liberty, at least by comparison with authoritarian regimes which invest their officials with discretionary power to punish political dissidents whose activities are "not in the public interest". Yet as early as 1890 one textbook on English criminal law stated as a fact that the conspiracy law "leaves so much discretion in the hands of the judges that it is hardly too much to say that plausible reasons may be found for declaring it to be a crime to do almost anything which the judges regard as morally wrong or politically or socially dangerous".

Lord Diplock, dissenting from the proposition that conspiracy to corrupt public morals still had a place in English law, complained that if it did, no citizen could make moral decisions involving another with certainty that he would not be prosecuted. Successive governments have closed their ears to such protests — perhaps because the conspiracy law is a useful stick to threaten radicals, perhaps because the whole area has become too vast and complicated for anyone other than lawyers to understand and even they have difficulties. It took eight years before twelve eminent lawyers appointed by the Law Commission produced so much as a "working paper" on conspiracy law reform. When they ultimately did so, in June 1973, they argued that the whole "unlawful act" doctrine, which was largely responsible for Hain's prosecution, offended against the fundamental principle of certainty in the criminal law:

> "It seems to us not merely desirable, but obligatory that legal rules imposing serious criminal sanctions should be stated with the maximum clarity which the imperfect medium of language can attain. The offence of conspiring to do an unlawful act offends against that precept in two ways. First, it is impossible in some cases even to state the rules relating to the object of criminal agreements except in terms which are at best tautologous and unenlightening. Secondly, in those cases where at least a statement of the offence is possible, that statement covers such a wide range of conduct that it is impossible to decide whether an offence has been committed or not."

The working paper recommended that all conspiracies to do acts such as trespass, which are not criminal, but merely "unlawful" should be abolished.

The Law Commission's concern for the certainty of the criminal law is amply justified by the "public interest" test laid down by Lord Hailsham in the Sierra Leone Embassy case *(R v Kamara)* as the reason for punishing non-violent civil trespass. Who is to decide what is "in the public domain" or, as Judge Gillis put it in the Peter Hain trial, what is "something of importance to citizens who are interested in the maintenance of law and order"? The Court of Appeal in the Sierra Leone case was aware of this difficulty:

> "If the public interest is to be considered, as counsel for the Crown suggested, who is to decide what it is? The Judge? Or the jury? Are either competent? Should evidence be admitted on this issue? If not, why not? If the judge is to decide, he may well take the verdict from the jury; if the jury is to decide, part of the law of conspiracy can be stated in four words: 'salus populi, suprema lex'."

The House of Lords reserved this decision for the judge, which means in practice that "public interest" questions will be decided by the prejudices of an elderly conservative quite out of touch with the public whose interest he will be called upon to divine. For example, Judge Gillis had no difficulty in rejecting Peter Hain's submission that Test matches with South Africa were not in the public interest because they would strain race relations in England. No doubt most judges can be relied upon to instruct their juries that the disruption of sporting fixtures and the defaming of visiting Portuguese dictators are matters of vital public concern, while a conspiracy to occupy the offices of *Release* or to defame Father Adrian Hastings, would lack the ingredient of public interest necessary to justify a criminal law. How, for example, did Judge Gillis divine that it was a matter of public concern to play cricket matches against South Africa? He completely ignored the political repercussions, and struck a Kiplingesque pose: "The game of cricket is the most English of English past-times . . . it has been played on our village greens for over 250 years . . ."

134

Occasionally the continued existence of these vague, dragnet charges is defended on the grounds that although they could be absurdly oppressive if vigorously enforced, for example if every couple who agreed to park illegally were jailed for conspiring to contravene the Road Traffic Act, the prosecuting authorities use common sense and only enforce the conspiracy law against conduct deserving punishment. But police have an obligation to investigate and prosecute all provable cases where a serious crime has been committed: not to do so would be a dereliction of duty. To argue that a serious criminal offence should only be prosecuted in certain blatant cases is to abandon the rule of law to the rule of police value-judgements. As Lord Reid has pointed out "a bad law is not defensible on the ground that it will be judiciously administered". In any case, as Francis Bennion so eloquently demonstrated, every citizen has a constitutional right to initiate a prosecution for criminal conspiracy. This leaves vague laws at the mercy of manipulation by cranks, bigots or people with a vested interest in silencing critics. Amongst the latter may be counted the wealthy white South Africans who subscribed to the "Pain for Hain" campaign.

The process of sentencing a convicted conspirator is also crippled by uncertainty, especially in complicated cases where he may only be guilty of agreeing to one insignificant "unlawful act", but is nevertheless sentenced as though he hatched the entire plot. Lawyers were able to dissect the first count of the Hain indictment into 147 different "unlawful activities". Were the jury to decide that Hain had committed only one of them, e.g., that he agreed to shine a mirror in a player's eyes, this would not be revealed from the foreman's monosyllabic grunt of "guilty". So the judge could sentence Hain on the basis that he had agreed to 146 other unlawful activities. This was emphasized when Hain, convicted of conspiring to disrupt a tennis match in a number of different ways, complained "I am still not certain of which particular I was found guilty". "You have not been convicted of a particular, but of a conspiracy" replied Judge Gillis.

In the first 'Angry Brigade' trial, Jake Prescott was sentenced to 15 years imprisonment – an appropriate term had he actively participated in all the bombings. Yet the conspiracy verdict was consistent with a jury finding that he had merely posted three 'Angry Brigade' letters to *The Times* – conduct deserving of a suspended sentence or at most a short jail term. This built-in unfairness in conspiracy charges embarrassed the authorities when the 'Stoke Newington 4', alleged to be much more centrally involved in the bomb plots, were jailed for 10 years and Prescott's sentence had to be reduced in consequence. Although most statutory offences have a maximum penalty, the punishment for conspiracy is "at large", giving the judges an absolute discretion and police a convenient way of subverting the intentions of Parliament when it approved a particular maximum limit. Recently, for example, pornographers have been charged with "conspiracy to contravene the Post Office Act" rather than with an offence against the Act itself, merely to enable judges to jail them for longer periods than the maximum provided in the Act. At Shrewsbury, Denis Warren was jailed for 3 years for conspiring to contravene legislation which itself carried a maximum penalty of only 3 months.

The conspiracy device is ideal for scapegoat prosecutions. The wide definition of "agreement" can place in the same dock defendants who have hitherto been unaware of each other's existence. Several of the 24 Shrewsbury building workers met for the first time in the police cells: they were selected from a picket line of 300 by such fortuitous factors as their identification from press and TV films of the demonstration. Now every person who joins a picket line risks a conspiracy prosecution for the simple reason that the necessary "agreement" can be inferred from the mere fact of his attendance. It matters not that the picketing is peaceful: as Mr. Robert Carr explained to Parliament "sheer numbers attending can of itself constitute intimidation". At Shrewsbury, much of the agitation was sparked off by an employer who threatened pickets with a loaded shotgun, yet this provocation was irrelevant to their guilt of conspiracy to intimidate.

Peter Hain was singled out from thousands of demonstrators against sporting apartheid: his public image made him a suitable scapegoat, although the prosecution knew the identity of others who were actually responsible for committing the "unlawful acts" which Hain was alleged to have countenanced. The classic use of conspiracy to convict scapegoats representing a mass movement was the trial of the Chicago 7, who had nothing in common except their presence in Chicago for the Democratic Convention. Hayden was an anti-war radical, Dellinger an old-fashioned pacifist, Hoffman an extrovert yippie, Davis a studious post-graduate who read chemistry textbooks during Rubin's courtroom antics, and so on. They all suffered guilt by association, but their "agreement" to do unlawful acts simply did not exist, except in cloud-cuckoo conspiracy land. "We can't even agree on lunch" complained an exasperated Abbie Hoffman when he took the stand.

Modern democratic political theory has it that Government depends on the consent of the governed, and obedience is owed to laws passed or approved by a majority of elected representatives. In the seventeenth century, when conspiracy was "moulded into an engine of Government", Parliament met infrequently and was in any case subservient to the Sovereign. It was convenient in this age that the King's Judges should develop the criminal law on a case-by-case basis, punishing new forms of wickedness as they arose. But the subsequent development of the law-making role of Parliament, to the point reached today where it meets with sufficient regularity to legislate against any undesirable conduct, makes it unnecessary as well as unconstitutional for judges to wield a power to make new criminal laws, or to stretch existing laws to cover novel situations. While politicians are drawn from all strata of society and are despatched to Westminster as representatives with a mandate to legislate, judges are invariably elderly men who have lived a socially isolated life, and whose desire to enforce moral values may not accurately reflect those of many sections of the community.

Moreover, laws which originate in Parliament are subjected to scrutiny by expert draftsmen and lawyers, to parliamentary debate and amendment, to submissions from interested bodies, to public criticism and to publicity, warning potential offenders of the penalty in store. But developments in the conspiracy laws are noted only in dusty volumes of law reports quite inaccessible to the general public. And this "judicial legislation" has other drawbacks. There is the difficulty and uncertainty of extrapolating any clear legal rule from up to five lengthy judgements. There is the danger of making law in a vacuum, impervious to social needs and the will of the people. And then there is the inevitable colouring given to the law by those who make it, Judges 'each of whom' Lord Diplock has himself been moved to admit, 'has his personal idiosyncrasies or sentiment and upbringing, not to speak of age'. Judges hardly possess the qualifications for making laws which will answer the needs and receive the approval of the community as a whole.

The classic example of how conspiracy lends itself to judicial manipulation in order to by-pass the law-making role of Parliament is the crime of conspiracy to trespass, revived first by Freedom Under Law Limited and then by the Director of Public Prosecutions to save the country from swarms of squatters, sitters-in and Springbok-stoppers. When 'sit-ins' and disruption of sporting fixtures became regular occurences in the late 1960s, tougher legislation was frequently advocated inside and outside Parliament, but in the event no action was taken. Even the Society of Conservative Lawyers, which appointed a working party under Sir Derek Walker-Smith QC to study the situation, decided in 1970 that no additional legislation was necessary. In reaching this conclusion, they assumed that "conspiracy to trespass" did not exist in English law. Their report, 'Public Order', specifically considered "The creation of an offence of criminal trespass . . . a new criminal offence in what has hitherto been a part of the civil law. It may be that circumstances and the development of militancy and other violent techniques could make such a change necessary. But for the purpose of this study we would prefer, for the time being, to consider this as a card of last resort which may, however, have to be played if circumstances should so require". They contemplated, of course, that the "card of last resort" would be played from a flush conservative parliamentary hand, and not from up a flushed conservative Lord Chancellor's ermine sleeve.

But on 4 July, 1973, Lord Hailsham and three judicial colleagues, in order to legitimise the police action against the Sierra Leone students and, indirectly, FUL action against Hain, discovered the existence of a law which in effect provides "It shall be an offence, the maximum punishment for which shall be life imprisonment, for two or more persons to agree to trespass upon the property of another, in cases where, in the opinion of the trial judge, the agreement is sufficiently a matter of public concern to come within the ambit of the criminal law". Had Mr Heath attempted to convince the House of Commons, or indeed the Society of Conservative Lawyers, that the country urgently required a Public Order Bill which provided such drastic penalties for minor breaches of the civil law, his efforts would have been bitterly fought and widely derided as a panic measure designed to crush the robust expression of genuine grievances. Lord Hailsham has defended the continued use of conspiracy charges on the grounds that "I personally prefer a bit of common law which is furry at the edges". But his control over conspiracy laws with furry edges during the 1970-74 Conservative Government enabled him to fashion that fur into hairshirts for those whose political activities he abominates, without the slightest reference to elected representatives or public debate, but merely the support of this other Law Lords from a panel for the most part as reactionary as himself. When he handed down judgement in the Sierra Leone Embassy case, 'conspiracy to trespass' became the law of the land as decidedly as if it had been unanimously passed on the third reading of the Public Order (Suppression of Free Speech and

Political Protest) Act 1973.

There are three fundamental precepts of criminal law in a democratic society its meaning and scope should be reasonably clear, it should express the will of the elected representatives of the people, and its procedure should conform to accepted standards of fairness. The conspiracy charge traduces each of these precepts. In the first place, certainty in the criminal law is prized because it enables a citizen to order his conduct so as to avoid transgressions: it is his right to know in what situations executive power may be marshalled against him. 'The Rule of Law' should set definite limits beyond which those in authority cannot pass in harassing political opponents. The rule of the conspiracy law, however, is so uncertain that judges and prosecuting authorities act as pile-drivers, staking out the bounds of criminality as it suits them, from case to case.

In the second place, orthodox democratic theory has it that government depends on the consent of the governed, and obedience is only owed to laws approved by the majority of elected representatives. Lord Reid has warned that "Where Parliament fears to tread it is not for the courts to rush in". Yet rush in they have, "developing the common law" by stretching the elastic principles of conspiracy to punish activities which they and the Director of Public Prosecutions deplore, but which Parliament has never seen fit to legislate against. Such a subversion of the legislative process might have been justified in the seventeenth century, when Parliament met infrequently and the task of law-making was entrusted to judges, who punished new forms of wickedness as they arose. The conspiracy law is a bitter but tenacious legacy of Star Chamber methods, which has outlived its purpose in an age where Parliament meets and legislates regularly. There is no longer any place for judicial law-making: the scope of 'public interest' and 'public morals' should be declared by the representatives of the public, and not by elderly members of an upper-class elite.

Finally, the tactical advantages reserved for the prosecution in a conspiracy case destroy the accused's right to a fair trial. It is often much easier to prove an agreement than it is to prove participation in the completed crime. Evidence which would be inadmissable were the defendant actually charged with committing the crime may be received to suggest that he agreed to commit it. And if the defendant is charged with both conspiracy and with the completed crime, then even if he is acquitted of conspiracy some of the otherwise inadmissable mud thrown pursuant to it may stick, so that the jury, prejudiced by what they have heard about the defendant's lifestyle and associates, may be satisfied with less than conclusive proof of his guilt on the other charges. The crowning unfairness is that a man convicted of conspiracy to commit a crime may be given any sentence his trial judge thinks fit — even if the statutory maximum punishment for the actual crime is no more than a small fine.

The danger posed to society by the existence of a dragnet law which lacks certainty, democratic origins and procedural fairness, is potentially very grave. It authorises trial and imprisonment of critics of conventional authority and value systems, in the same way as 'public safety' legislation bolsters executive tyranny in communist and fascist countries. Of course, whether it is so used depends upon the discretion of prosecuting authorities and judges: but the fact that they have used that discretion with some degree of common sense in the past is no guarantee that they will do so in future, and certainly is no justification for the existence of the discretion in the first place. Emergency powers should be voted by Parliament only in emergencies, and not used as a device for punishing those whose politics embarrasses the Establishment. Being "done for conspiracy" increasingly means being no more than a victim of police suspicion, or of being a person who, for reasons of politics or lifestyle, the police wish to harass or silence, but are unable to do so by proving the actual commission of a crime. Public scepticism, which breeds at grass-roots among young people whose friends are victims of "conspiracy to possess cannabis" charges, is reinforced on a national scale by disquiet at the use of conspiracy laws in political 'show' trials such as those involving the underground press, anti-apartheid demonstrators and trade union pickets. It has generated a nightmarishly complicated set of precedents and principles, described by Lord Diplock recently as "the least sympathetic, the most irrational branch of the English penal law". As its leading academic critic, Professor Sayre, concludes, "A doctrine so vague in its outlines and uncertain in its fundamental nature as criminal conspiracy lends no strength or glory to the law, it is a veritable quicksand of shifting opinion and ill-considered thought".

In 1973 the Law Commission, a body of eminent lawyers charged with recommending legal reforms the the Government, emphatically condemned some of the developments in the law which had made the Hain case possible, arguing that "a law of conspiracy extending beyond the ambit of conspiracy to commit crimes has, in our view, no place in a comprehensively planned criminal code". In consequence, it advocated abolition of the old "unlawful act" doctrine, so that agreements to commit civil wrongs, such as trespass, libel, or breach of contract cannot be punished as though they were serious criminal offences. These civil wrongs can usually be redressed by individual victims suing for damages, without the intercession of the criminal law. The "public interest" is much too subjective and uncertain to serve as an authorisation for aggressive police intrusion into the private domain. If the Government feels that squatters and sitters-in constitute a danger to society rather than a temporary inconvenience to property developers and private institutions, it should have the courage to propose specific criminal legislation, clear in scope and with maximum penalties, rather than to rely upon judges to "develop the common law" stealthily in the desired direction, without the consent of Parliament. Until the conspiracy law is reformed on the lines suggested by the Law Commission, it will remain a bewildering and frightening Pandora's box, its key available not only to the Government but, as the Hain prosecution demonstrated, to private prosecutors who can afford the price.